Dynamism and its Enemies

For permission requests, contact:
The Civitas Institute at the University of Texas at Austin
civitas@utexas.edu

ISBN: 979-8-218-63816-0

Cover design: Allison Smythe
Edited by: Ryan Streeter

Printed in the United States of America. First Edition: 2025

Dynamism and its Enemies

Contributor Bios

Ryan Decker is the chief of the Industrial Output Section at the Federal Reserve Board. His past and present internal Board responsibilities have included serving as a special adviser to Governor Adriana Kugler; coordinating the staff G.D.P. forecast; tracking the industrial sector especially motor vehicles, aircraft, and oil and gas; and working on various small/new business and nontraditional data projects. He is also a member of the Conference on Research in Income and Wealth, and a Special Sworn Status researcher at the U.S. Census Bureau.

Edward L. Glaeser is the Fred and Eleanor Glimp Professor of Economics at Harvard University. He leads the Urban Economics Working Group at the National Bureau of Economics Research, co-leads the Cities Programme of the International Growth Centre, and co-edits the *Journal of Urban Economics.* Glaeser has written hundreds of papers on cities, infrastructure and other topics, and has written, co-written, and co-edited several books including *Triumph of the City, Survival of the City*, and *Fighting Poverty in the U.S. and Europe: A World of Difference.* He has served as director of the Taubman Center for State and Local Government and the Rappaport Institute for Greater Boston, editor of the *Quarterly Journal of Economics*, and chair of Harvard's economics department. Glaeser received his A.B. from Princeton University and his Ph.D. in economics from the University of Chicago.

Deirdre Nansen McCloskey is a senior fellow and holder of the Isaiah Berlin Chair in Liberal Thought at the Cato Institute in Washington, D.C. She is an emerita distinguished professor of economics and history, emerita professor of English and communication, and emerita adjunct professor of classics and philosophy at the University of Illinois at Chicago. She also taught for twelve years in the department of economics at the University of Chicago. Trained at Harvard as an economist, she has written twenty-five books and edited nine more, and has published some five hundred articles on economic history, economic theory, statistical theory, rhetoric, literary criticism, feminism, epistemology, ethics, academic policy, legal theory, and liberalism.

Edmund Phelps, the winner of the 2006 Nobel Prize in Economics, is director of the Center on Capitalism and Society at Columbia University. After a stint at RAND, he held positions at Yale and its Cowles Foundation, a professorship at Penn, and finally a professorship at Columbia. He has written books on growth, unemployment theory, recessions, stagnation, inclusion, rewarding work, dynamism, indigenous innovation, and the good economy, including *Mass Flourishing* (2013). He earned his B.A. from Amherst and Ph.D. at Yale.

Daniel Shoag is a visiting associate professor at the Weatherhead School of Management. He is an associate professor of public policy at Harvard Kennedy School and an affiliate of the Taubman Center for State and Local Government. His research focuses on state and local government finance, worker signaling and the hiring process, and regional and urban economics. Shoag's research has been published in major academic journals and has been featured, among other outlets, in *The New York Times*, *Bloomberg*, *The Washington Post*, and *The Wall Street Journal*. Shoag has worked as a visiting scholar at the Federal Reserve Bank of Boston, a visiting professor at Tel Aviv University, and was selected as a rising new scholar by the Stanford University Center on Poverty and Inequality. He received his B.A. and Ph.D. in economics from Harvard University.

Ryan Streeter is executive director of the Civitas Institute. Previously, he was the State Farm James Q. Wilson Scholar and director of domestic policy studies at the American Enterprise Institute (AEI), where he facilitated research in education, technology, housing, urban policy, poverty studies, workforce development, and public opinion. Before joining AEI, he was executive director of the Center for Politics and Governance at UT Austin. He is the author, coauthor, and editor of six books, including *Doing Right by Kids: Leveraging Social Capital* and *Innovation to Increase Opportunity* which he co-edited with Scott Winship and Yuval Levin, and T*he Future of Cities*, which he co-edited with Joel Kotkin. His writings have appeared in *The Washington Post*, *The Wall Street Journal*, *The Atlantic*, *Politico*, *USA Today*, *The Hill*, *City Journal*, *National Affairs*, and *National Review*, among others. He has a Ph.D. in political philosophy from Emory University.

Cass R. Sunstein is currently the Robert Walmsley University Professor at Harvard. He is the founder and director of the Program on Behavioral Economics and Public Policy at Harvard Law School. In 2018, he received the Holberg Prize from the government of Norway, sometimes described as the equivalent of the Nobel Prize for law and the humanities. In 2020, the World Health Organization appointed him as chair of its technical advisory group on Behavioural Insights and Sciences for Health. He is author of hundreds of articles and dozens of books. He served as senior counselor to the Secretary of Homeland Security during the Biden Administration and was awarded the Distinguished Public Service Medal, the Department's highest civilian honor, in 2024.

Introduction

Ryan Streeter

If we want more people in more places building and creating more good things, what should we do?

At times it seems that leaders of developed economies, such as ours in the United States, reject the question's premise. Much of the public discussion about economic growth focuses on productivity and employment measures but we hear less from public leaders about whether and how we are more innovative, entrepreneurial, and creative in more places around the country. Policymakers often act as if their job is to tweak elements of productivity and employment so that this month's G.D.P. and jobs reports look at least a little better than last month's.

Our leaders should instead be obsessed with answering the opening question rather than maintaining the economic policy status quo. Why? Because many more people would find meaning in their work, fulfill their potential, and yes, earn more money. When we do not see what we are missing out on, we often think things are going well.

But "good enough" is not good enough. We need to reckon with some important realities. New businesses' positive effect on job growth is well-documented, and yet despite an encouraging recent surge in entrepreneurial activity (for reasons not yet fully known), the share of startup-created jobs has declined by about a third over the past generation. We simply are not as entrepreneurial as we tell ourselves we are. We are also less mobile than in the past, as people choose to stay put rather than move to opportunity-rich places. A key culprit in declining mobility, the housing regulations that drive up house prices, also significantly reduce G.D.P. through the lost productivity that comes with immobility. Housing regulations and immobility have cascading effects that lead to other problems such as fewer startups, less job-hopping, and even declining fertility rates. Decreasing dynamism also negatively affects job satisfaction. Workers in places with high innovation levels and marked by values such as openness and creativity have higher job satisfaction levels, but job satisfaction has experienced a remarkable decline over time in too many places.

Declining entrepreneurship, less mobility, and low levels of job satisfaction are signs of a stagnating society. Their opposites—people moving to opportunity, more people starting new businesses, more housing production, more people job-hopping for more earnings and more meaningful work—characterize a dynamic society.

The word dynamism derives from the Greek word *dunamis,* or power. It connotes not merely strength or force but the energy and ability something has to fulfill its potential.

An economy that is dynamic is more than a growing economy. G.D.P. that increases at a higher rate this quarter than last quarter is a good thing for multiple reasons, but it measures dynamism incompletely. Dynamism should be understood more broadly than in purely economic terms: people taking risks to create new businesses, people daring to buck with convention to create a better way to do something, people picking up and moving to a new opportunity even if it involves homesickness, people with a sufficient level of resilience to try again when they fail.

I used the word "people" repeatedly in the previous sentence to emphasize the point that dynamic societies begin first and foremost with the values and habits of the people that comprise them. Over time, if a society—through its government policies, cultural norms, business practices, and educational institutions—makes dynamic activity too hard and too risky, people will become less dynamic themselves. As Nobel laureate and contributor to this volume Edmund Phelps has shown, formerly dynamic societies can change their population's nature over time such that a previously adventurous and experimental culture is lost.

The United States's dynamism stands out globally—from its share of small companies that have grown into more than $1 billion enterprises to the amount of innovation investment—but this masks wide swathes of stagnation around the country. Many more people in more places could, and should, be making more good things.

The chapters in *Dynamism and Its Enemies* began as presentations at the 2024 Austin Symposium, a one-day seminar on dynamism in America hosted by the Civitas Institute at the University of Texas at Austin. This first annual event, held in one of America's most dynamic cities, was designed to bring various leading scholars of dynamism's various aspects into one place in order to think together about how to answer this introduction's opening question.

Our hope is that this book's ideas will inspire others to pursue inquiry into the questions we leave unanswered and to encourage decision-makers such as policymakers, business leaders, investors, and civic leaders to craft ideas for removing barriers to dynamic activity and the creative endeavors a dynamic future requires.

True to the idea that dynamism is more than a narrow economic concept, this book covers new business creation, housing, migration, regulatory barriers to dynamism, and the history of how vibrant and flourishing societies came to be.

Deirdre McCloskey's account of the remarkable origins of the current cornucopia of wealth and opportunity that we often take for granted, which the 18th century's prioritization of natural liberty made possible, opens our volume. She describes how an "equality of permission" in a bottom-up liberal state creates the conditions for the experimentation, effort, and productivity that produce human flourishing on a scale that top-down liberal regimes threaten to undo.

To understand what makes a society dynamic, we need to look beyond purely economic explanations. Edmund Phelps describes how modern societies began to reward the creativity and vitalism that lead to mass flourishing. Indigenous innovation that arose in places where new ideas and experimental methods abounded led not only to increases in material wealth but also more meaningful and satisfying jobs for working people. Phelps cautions that the rise of a "money culture" in advanced societies portends stagnation and decline as incentives shift away from the joy of creation and working in interesting jobs to having things and status as ends in themselves.

Governments in advanced economies that have benefited from growth and innovation create regulatory guardrails to minimize creative destruction's destructive aspects. But what happens when those guardrails become so numerous and inflexible that they also reduce a dynamic economy's creative aspects? Ed Glaeser and Cass Sunstein have spent years analyzing what we lose when the accrual of regulatory restrictions reduces dynamic activity.

Glaeser's chapter is a *tour de force* of examples of how too much government regulation, on the one hand, and too little government efficiency on the other inhibits dynamism. Glaeser examines why some cities have the resilience to endure and thrive through large economic shocks while others decline. He explores the building blocks of adaptability and how the interplay of regulation, education, openness, and efficiency creates a pro-dynamism environment, while over-regulation—however well-intended for this or that good cause—and a failure to appreciate the mobility of people and capital leads to stagnation and decline.

Sunstein demonstrates how regulatory sludge and cognitive scarcity combine to prohibit the innovation and pace of growth we need to lead flourishing lives. The cost of compliance and hours spent on paperwork and processes robs innovators, entrepreneurs, small business owners, ambitious young people, and other strivers of opportunities that would benefit not only them but the rest of us. Sunstein looks at a variety of ways that sludge can be reduced or mitigated, from changing incentive structures to goals-based reductions in time and rules to extending permitting timelines. Sunstein's chapter is a handbook for reform-minded policymakers at all levels of government.

There are other factors beyond regulatory intervention in the economy that negatively affect dynamism, and nothing showcases them more than the decades-long trend in declining startups in America. For years, the share of new businesses compared to all businesses has been shrinking, and economists have offered multiple reasons why. Unexpectedly, this trend reversed during the coronavirus pandemic. Ryan Decker's data-packed chapter showcases his new and original research on what might explain the recent new business creation surge, and how we might think about it in light of the various explanations for startups' long-term downward trend. It is too early to tell if the pandemic's startup surge marks the beginning of a new trend, but Decker's chapter is the starting point for others who want to continue to explore this question.

There is perhaps no issue as significant as housing in terms of flawed policies' cascading effects. When aspiring workers and business owners cannot afford to live near opportunity, everyone loses. They lose out on opportunity and the area in which they would like to live is deprived of their productivity and creativity. Declining geographic mobility has a direct downward effect on economic dynamism. Dan Shoag does a deep dive into the reasons why housing prices grow, with land-use and zoning practices taking center stage. He documents how getting housing policy wrong causes economic losses and offers policymakers a range of data points to help them understand how better to align homebuyers, developers, and government officials' incentives.

Dynamism has many enemies: housing restrictions, labor policy, safety guidelines, compliance rules, and many other barriers to creativity, innovation, and adventure. Dynamism's friends are those adventurists, problem-solvers, builders, and innovators at all levels of our society whose work creates better opportunities for other people to fulfill their potential. Our hope is that this book's ideas will help policymakers and other decision-makers do more to address the former in service of the latter. If they do, a dynamic future awaits.

Endnotes

[1]Ryan Decker, John Haltiwanger, Ron Jarmin, Javier Miranda, "The Role of Entrepreneurship in US Job Creation and Economic Dynamism," *Journal of Economic Perspectives*, vol. 28, no. 3 (2014). https://www.aeaweb.org/articles?id=10.1257/jep.28.3.3

[2]See Chang-Tai Hsieh and Enrico Moretti, "Housing Constraints and Spatial Misallocation," *American Economic Journal: Macroeconomics* 2019, 11 (2): 1-39.

[3]Edmund Phelps with Raicho Bojilov, Hian Teck Hoon, and Gylfi Zoega, *Dynamism: The Values that Drive Innovation, Job Satisfaction and Economic Growth* (Cambridge, MA: Harvard University Press, 2020).

[4]This book's title is a not-so-subtle acknowledgement of Virginia Postrel's seminal *The Future and Its Enemies*, which artfully identified the forces of stagnation more than twenty-five years ago and laid the groundwork for more inquiry into the sources of dynamism.

Part I
The History and Nature
of Dynamic Societies

1. The Great Enrichment

Deirdre Nansen McCloskey

New and old assaults on liberalism have taught us that good politics depends not so much on institutions as it does on the moral sentiments supporting the institutions. "Add institutions and stir" is not a recipe for success. If malicious people take over a nation by coup or by vote, no structure of institutions, such as the American Constitution, can help—at least not much. On the other hand, enough of the great and good can make any ramshackle institution, such as the British constitution, work pretty well.

After all, for better or for worse, ethical principles run any human group, ranging from a conversation, a marriage, or relationships among a few friends, up to a sports team, a business, or a state. Meaningful conversations depends on Gricean maxims. A good marriage depends on love, respect, or both. A sports team depends on team spirit. A well-functioning business depends on intrinsic motivations. A successful gang of thieves depends on *omertà*. Well-designed laws, catechisms, extrinsic incentives, supreme courts, social approvals, traditional formulas, and even upstanding leaders are straws in the wind if too many people are not self-respecting, other-respecting, and value-respecting adults. The functioning of institutions, laws, catechisms, incentives, courts, approvals, formulas, and chosen leaders reflect the people's character.

For millennia, the moral sentiments of proud aristocrats and deferential subjects ruled most large societies. The result was stifled creativity in the contemptible mess of the people. Economic historians in present-day prices calculate that the average human being since the caves lived on $2/day. Then, all of a sudden after 1776, it shot up in liberal countries. Yet by 1960, four out of Earth's five billion people still lived in the $2/day misery of rags, hovels, and campfires. One out of eight billion still do today. Meanwhile, the worldwide daily average in the same prices has exploded to $50/day.

In November 1790, Edmund Burke lamented the old dispensation's twilight. "The age of chivalry is gone," he said, "that of sophisters, oeconomists, and calculators has succeeded; and the glory of Europe is extinguished forever." His beloved age of the Great Chain of Being, a naturalized hierarchy—which Burke praised in the same passage as leading to "freedom" through subornation to rank—slowly gave way to our liberal, plebeian age. By now, rank no longer counts.

But two different liberalisms emerged, based on contending sentiments and on different factual judgments about how best to achieve prosperity, equality, and true liberty. First, a bottom-up liberalism of personal and unpredictable liberty, and second, a top-down liberalism of social and predictable construction. In 1776, Adam Smith declared for "the obvious and simple system of natural liberty," a spontaneous, bottom-up order like a language. Yet in that same propitious year for liberalism, Thomas Paine declared that "we have it in our power to begin the world again," with imposed, from-the-top order, like engineering. By now, most political philosophers, oeconomists, and calculators have come to advocate liberalism that is top-down in aid of the general will.

I myself am one of the oeconomists and calculators. But I have grown suspicious of my fellow economists' top-down schemes, which I now believe are based on non-economics and non-calculation. Over the past couple of decades I've claimed to have shown the non-nesses factually and conceptually. Fundamentally, the top-down schemes depend on a persistent but impossible modernist dream: that a simple machine like a Turing machine or a monetary rule of a production function can successfully predict complex systems such as the weather, the English language, the evolution of species, or the economy's functioning.[1] The dream is Comte's: to know in order to predict and to predict in order to control. This is easily accomplished, said the state's engineers, with simple input and output systems, if you merely have a large enough computer. Statists therefore believe we should have a central plan, a central bank, a central mind in charge of running the Turing machine. Everything is simple, centralized, intentional, and engineered. Let's get organized to help the poor. It's simple. Or we should get organized to invade Vietnam. It's simple.

I claim that an economy or a polity, like an art, science, or the course of true love, is ill-described as an input-output system with its simple, one-to-one, function-like results. Human liberty and creativity lead to complex systems, non-Turing machines, that are chaotically unpredictable after a few steps into the future. Before Edward Lorenz developed such theories about a startling sensitivity to initial conditions in predicting the weather in the 1970s, the economists Ludwig von Mises in the 1930s and Friedrich Hayek in the 1940s had made the same point about the economy. The bulk of economic, political, and social engineers didn't listen.

Even the Blessed Smith didn't quite grasp how explosive, how very non-linearly dynamic, and how non-routine the liberal implementation of his idea of "the obvious and simple system of natural liberty" would prove to be. Despite tyrants' attempts to suppress it—yet also despite the unintended consequences of amiable New Liberals with their statist schemes—income per person in real terms during the two-and-a-half centuries after 1776 rose from the misery of $2/day worldwide to the modest comforts of $50/day, and to the luxury of well over $100/day in an increasing number of counties. The growth from $2/day to $50/day is a gob-smacking, utterly unpredicted, and a seemingly permanent 2,500 percent increase per person. Its magnitude points to an unprecedented ideological cause: human language in aid of non-linear dynamics, not the routine input-output material causes long suggested, such as slavery or investment, imperialism or trade. It amply justifies my own neologisms of "innovism" for the tired and inaccurate "capitalism" and "the Great Enrichment" for the tired and inaccurate "industrial revolution." If we don't mess it up with too much regulation, too much redistribution, or too much war—all of which destroy liberal innovism—the average human being's income is on schedule to rise during the next century to $400/day per person, more than twice the current Swiss income. Praise the Lord, and liberty.

I have slowly over the writing of my long books, from 2006 to the present, become persuaded that a virtuous and effective liberalism, with its astonishing fruit in material and spiritual flourishing, depends on an equality of *permission*. Only equality of permission leads to substantial equality of real comfort. More state coercions, which promise but do not come close to achieving material equalities, do not achieve this liberalism. What our 18th-century forebears proposed was a "mere" liberalism. That first liberalism was the correct one, and it suffices. Only such an equality of mere respect conduces to universal human flourishing.

By contrast, the later Jacobins advocated state coercion in order to impose material equality directly. Still later in liberalism's history, that became the conventional wisdom, as it did for our beloved but self-contradicting J. S. Mill. It did not work. Meanwhile the mere equality of permission proposed in July 1776, and August 1789—not Mill's quasi-socialism and frank imperialism—which raised up adult citizens and liberated them to have a go, turned out tin in the long run to achieve material equalities worldwide.

Statism does neither. Statism is the opposite of liberalism—though since the 1880s it has cannily appropriated for its concerns the honored L-word. Subsequent state attempts to impose material outcome or opportunity equality did not achieve their promises even approximately, because they nurtured societies filled with childlike serfs. Recent states' greatly enhanced capacity to monitor and punish their subjects works pretty well if its rulers are decent people, like a Roosevelt or a Jimmy Carter. But meanwhile, statism arms tyrants, like a Huey Long or a Leonid Brezhnev. The "New" Liberals have quite recently learned, as perhaps they should have learned from the 20th century's nightmares, that absolute power corrupts absolutely.

As I said, good moral sentiments need to support any liberal ideology. By any definition, most liberals already possess good moral sentiments—as for that matter do the conservatives whom I admire. I do not adopt the left and right's easy trope of supposing that people who disagree with me about good politics have bad will. But the democratic socialists, progressive quasi-liberals, and compassionate conservatives' good will has lost its way. All of these good people have rushed past historical evidence, economic logic, and *Federalist* 10, in a belief that good intentions and a pure heart armed with centralized coercions do suffice to raise up our fellow human beings. They don't.

In 1950, the great "liberal"—by his time the word had already settled into the strange U.S. sense—Lionel Trilling admitted that the danger is that "we who are liberal and progressive know that the poor are our equals in every sense except that of being equal to us." The same may be said of Burkeans and other conservatives, then and now. Trilling wrote that "we must be aware of the dangers that lie in our most generous wishes," because "when once we have made our fellow men the object of our enlightened interest [we] go on to make them the objects of our pity, then of our wisdom, ultimately of our coercion."

I claim that implementing instead a mere, minimal, but universally applied equality of permission does suffice. Its partial implementation since 1776 it has shown its sufficiency most spectacularly. It is precisely Smith's "obvious and simple" system of respect for oneself, for other people, and for a sweet and liberal transcendent—a transcendent of art or baseball or God—when they are in fact sweet and liberal. Transcendents break bad when they are the White Race or the German Nation or the One True Faith or Our Progressive Wisdom, or merely the Excellent Profits From Screwing You. We've seen how those work out. But even the transcendents of helping the poor or managing the economy—saintly or at least understandable if the economy was a simple system—have broken bad, from the Terror to the Bolsheviks, from Lady Bountiful to the New Deal. They have become careless of equality of permission, the first and essential liberalism. Equality of permission has been in historical fact the sole path to the Great Enrichment that does not corrupt and a substantial material equality of outcome and opportunity. An egalitarian should support essential liberalism, only.

Belief in that "statism" is the underlying reason that modern politics in its implementation breaks bad. It is the ancient and now universal conviction that top-down rather than bottom-up does the job of human flourishing so much more promptly and securely than mere liberal permission. Caesar believed it, and shattered the Roman Republic as a result. I do not use the word "statism" here as a vague insult against opponents. I try to use it scientifically, as a precise characterization of what many good-willed people, in politics left, right, and middle, have come to believe, especially over the past century. The widespread belief in statism is also what many people of bad will, left, right, and middle, have therefore been pleased to exploit. If I am correct, we will fail to achieve a good society until we become sharply aware of statism's dangers. Absorbed into a single tyrant, statism is Caesarism, or shall we say Putin-ism. But you should not suppose that a populist Parisian mob, a German scientific bureaucracy, or even a finely crafted American Constitution with separation of powers does liberty much better than a one-man tyrant does if a statism ideology prevails. If the mastering group directs a mighty modern state—a state taking a third to a half G.D.P., and regulating much of the rest, and therefore so very well worth corrupting—then liberty dies. Coercion becomes the order of the day, and equality of permission is lost in a new hierarchy. Said the party man O'Brien to Winston in *Nineteenth Eighty-Four*, "If you want a picture of the future, imagine a boot stamping on a human face—for ever."[2] You might reply that I'm exaggerating. But look around at Erdogan, Maduro, Crown Prince Mohammed bin Salman, Supreme Leader Ayatollah Ali Khamenei, Vladimir Putin, Xi Jinping, and Donald Trump.

Moral sentiments of liberal respect for self, others, and the good transcendents are learned at one's mother's knee. After mother, a good preacher, artists sometimes getting it right, or the very language we use habitually also teach us the republican virtues. Marcus Porcius Cato the Younger (d. 46 B.C.) and his nephew and son-in-law Marcus Junius Brutus (d. 42 B.C.) had listened intently to their mothers and the rest, as noble Romans had since the brave days of old. Gaius Julius Caesar (d. 44 B.C.) had not.

In Europe after 1790, reactionaries attacked the universal equality of an ethically constrained permission. They're still at it. Let us join together and overthrow them. But my central worry here is that after 1790, and in particular after 1848, the hard socialism or soft New Liberalism that are both still with us today widened their attacks against the first, novel, and essential liberalism. In the project of overthrowing the *ancien régime's* old hierarchies, the post-1848 pair of statist ideologies agreed with the older, if then still very young, essential liberalism. All three shared the appeal to banish the old masters. No to slavery. That's good.

Yet without thinking it through or attending to the observed results, the socialists and New Liberals proposed to install new, collective masters and new, elected tyrannies. Their favorite word became "collective," and from left and right they appealed for a masterful state to impose national unity and an imagined *volonté générale*. The modern European "nation state" as it came to be called, had from the 16th century slowly replaced the fragmented polity of what came to be called "feudalism." The first, essential liberalism was a criticism precisely of The State's new, masterful, centralized ideology. *The Wealth of Nations* is a sustained criticism of a mercantilism raised to a national policy. Essential liberalism arises from national statism.[3] The Jacobins of 1791 supplemented the mere, simple Declaration of the Rights of Man and the Citizen in 1789 with modest public education and poor relief redistributions. In the late 19th-century the Neo-Jacobins went a little further with redistribution, regulation, and public works. In the 20th a century the Neo-neo-Jacobins impended full-bore, neo-mercantilism on all sides.

They have a theory. They still indignantly ask the essential liberals: what does "liberty" mean if the state does not directly assure the material equalities? The bare liberty of permission, the statists claim, leads to terrible inequalities and other grave imperfections, including inequality, ethical horrors, monopoly, corruption, mass unemployment, irreligion, and anomie. They claimed that the Turing machine of state intervention can correct all such faults in the Turing machines of the economy, polity, and society. Admittedly, they can put forward no serious scientific evidence for the faults, never mind for the supposition that the economy, polity, society, or the correcting state is a Turing machine of input-output. That does not matter.

Let us engage in a bit of statism, or even quite a lot, if necessary. Let's provide the U.S. oldsters with socialized medicine and the South Asian poor with material capabilities. Let's provide and regulate electricity and water supply and plan town and country property. How otherwise can we prosper *equally*? In 1894 Anatole France wittily expressed the statist moral sentiments against mere legal equality of permission: "The law, in its majestic equality [being merely, first-liberal, Old-Whig], forbids rich and poor alike to sleep under bridges, to beg in the streets, and to steal their bread."

The supplementary equalities in housing, bread, health, and education were to be arranged top-down. What other method can assure material equality? Let us have a proletariat dictatorship, a New Deal, or a War on Poverty. After 1792 or 1848 or 1914 or 1917 or 1937 or 1945 or 1965, pick your year, the liberal—and many of the illiberal—states embarked on a steadily enlarging, social engineering project, top-down. We have begun the world again, *da capo*, for the best or the worst of motives. Our supervisors are good or bad statists in the line of Robespierre and Comte, Bismarck and the Roosevelts, Wilson and Keynes, Lenin and Mussolini, and today's numerous enthusiasts for what they now believe to be the very wise and very mighty state.

Has proliferating statisms, even in sweet New Liberalism's moderate form, been good for us or bad? We can answer this question scientifically by examining the evidence, and by framing the evidence ethically and philosophically. Perhaps the argument for essential liberalism's recovery and statism's curbing is worth a hearing. We shall see if it gets it.

Endnotes

[1] Smith and Landgrebe Smith, Barry, and Jobst Landgrebe. 2022. Why Machines Will Never Rule the World: Oxford and New York: Routledge. *Artificial Intelligence without Fear.*

[2] Orwell 1949, Chp. 3.

[3] A conversation with Alberto Mingardi clarified this point for me.

2. Reflections on *Mass Flourishing,* Ten Years Later

Edmund Phelps

I'm honored to be here at the University of Texas, Austin and to deliver the luncheon speech at today's Symposium. I want to thank Ryan Streeter, executive director of the Civitas Institute for inviting me to speak on dynamism — a topic I've been working on for the last two decades or so.

A New Theory of the Rise of Innovation

Seven years after my book *Mass Flourishing* (2013) introduced a new theory of innovation, I published with a team of researchers the sequel *Dynamism* (2020) which went on to test that theory. My new theory was that a key part of the widespread innovation found in several nations in the West derives from the outpouring of fresh *ideas* springing from the imagination and creativity of people working in these nation's businesses — most of them ordinary people, as I like to say.[1] (In familiar parlance, the supply of innovation per working person is a *function* of these people's expression of their creativity.) This theory of the supply of indigenous innovation is in sharp contrast to the theory advanced by the German Historical School, which held that innovations derived from discoveries made outside the economy and its businesses.

> The theory of *indigenous* innovating introduced here does *not throw away* the force of exogenous discoveries, which are present in the Solow-Swan model (and could be injected into the Keynes-Hicks model). The new theory injects *another force* into such macro models.

These new ideas pouring out of society came from a range of people, most of them having no experience experimenting in laboratories or exploring the great beyond. The renowned British historian Paul Johnson in his chronicle, *The Birth of the Modern* (1991), portrays many of the people whose inventiveness and determination produced the many innovations in Britain in the fifteen years from the end of the Napoleonic Wars in 1815 to 1830.[2] The noted Harvard economist Frank Taussig famously attributed the explosion of innovation in New England that he was studying to "Yankee ingenuity," not to scientists or explorers.[3] Many people in all walks of life were drawn in the firms where they worked to take part in the transformation going on. A romantic desire to join in these ground-breaking activities is conveyed in the film version of *Wuthering Heights* when Cathy cries out, "Go, Heathcliff. Bring back the world."

Yet *what accounts*, it might be asked, for the emergence of *aspirations* and *visions* leading to the flow of new methods and products? Of course, there had to be companies and sole proprietorships having a sense of *opportunities* in their industries for developing new methods and products. There had to be some sense of the size of the commercial demand for products. These desires and expectations determine the *demand* for innovation. (There are uses for this entrepreneurship, on which Schumpeter was so very focused.)

But what accounts for a society's supply of its *new ideas*? Evidently, the bubbling-up of these new ideas, which began in one nation after another over the 19th century, was fueled by newfound desires of people to create new ways and new things. Yet, it might be asked, why did such indigenous innovation, with its job satisfactions for many people and widespread productivity gains in most industries, *arise* in *these* nations while *not* in the *other* nations?

In the theory of this widespread innovating set out in *Mass Flourishing*, the *wellspring* of innovation was the desire to conceive new methods and new products. This reflected a newfound character among the people (or a great many of them): a character that had been *evolving* and *developing* in much of the West over two centuries and had *spread widely* among nationals by the middle of the 19th century. There was a willingness and desire to create new ways and new things.

Of course, such a development would not have been possible had there not been a rising number of people over the 17th and 18th centuries who grasped the

Renaissance idea (introduced by Pico della Mirandola at the end of the 16th century) that people are *born* with *some creativity*.[4] Thus, *ordinary* people came to understand that creating things was possible and might not be uncommon. But what stimulated many people working in the economy to make use of this creativity they (and others) had? What *drove* such a desire?

In this thesis of mine, the force driving people to conceive innovations was the rise and spread of certain *modern values* — *individualism, vitalism*, and a desire for *self-expression*. *Individualism* (not to be confused with selfishness) is the desire to have some independence — to make one's own way. Vitalism is the notion we feel alive when we are "acting on the world" (to use Hegel's term), when we take a chance and journey into the unknown. Self-expression is the gratification that comes from making use of our imagination and creativity — voicing one's thoughts or showing one's talents. In being *inspired* to imagine and create a new way or new thing people may reveal a part of who they are.

Mass Flourishing argues that a great many people, fueled by their innate creativity and driven by their modern values, were able and eager to engage in projects to create new ways or new things to make and sell — and many succeeded in their efforts. Consumers too were excited by the new goods. (In America, where innovation began exploding in the late 1850s, Abraham Lincoln, after his tour of the nation (prior to campaigning for the presidency), was struck at people's enthusiasm to see innovations sprouting up in stores and shops, and *exclaimed* that these people "have a passion — a *perfect rage* — for the new." [5])

By the 1880s in Britain and America, Germany, France and soon several more nations, a huge number of new products and methods were emerging from the business sector: *indigenous* innovations largely born of the new ideas hit upon by a wide number of participants in the business sector of the economy — not mainly the fruit of *exogenous* discoveries made by scientists and explorers. This huge outpouring of *indigenous* innovation conceived by modern people came to *dwarf* the exogenous innovation deriving from the discoveries of scientists and explorers.

In this new epoch with its modern spirit, *ordinary people* from the grassroots on up — not just scientists and explorers — had *original ideas*, a great many of which were conceived for commercial use. This was not altogether unprecedented. Human beings have been found to possess as long ago as the stone age the ability to create objects for use — *and* apparently the *need* to express their creativity.[6] (Of course, the desire or urge to engage in this activity — and the *opportunity* to do so — differed from country to country and from epoch to epoch.)

In the nations fueled by this new spirit, a *modern economy* formed: the typical industry had workers, managers, or other employees who, using their creativity, hit upon new ideas at one time or another. With this creativity, these nations had sufficient *dynamism* — the power and *desire* to innovate — and sufficient population — to generate a large flow of *indigenous* innovation.

Evidence for the New Theory of Innovation

Is there *evidence* for this theory of indigenous innovation? The book *Dynamism* published in 2020, which Raicho Bojilov, Hian Teck Hoon, Gylfi Zoega and I wrote, *tests* the new theory.

It first presents a set of data from 1890 to 1910 on the steep *rise* of cumulative *indigenous* innovation that began in the U.K., the U.S., France, Germany, and Italy — and then a set of data on the resumption of indigenous innovation in the U.S., France, and Italy from 1950 to 1972.[7] (The surge of U.S. innovation from 1995 to 2004 mostly occurred in Silicon Valley.)

What explains these twenty year explosions? *Conceivably*, this high innovation was a result of outpouring of *scientific discoveries* in the world, as Cassel and Spiethoff would have thought, or was the result of a *heightened willingness* among entrepreneurs to undertake the development of new ideas, as Schumpeter might have thought. *But* that theory does not explain at all well some striking data.

Calculations of data by Raicho Bojilov reveal that, for about a century, innovation was *consistently impressive* in some countries — and *consistently meager* in some others.[8] Over the postwar period of high innovation (comparable to the historic period from the 1870s to World War I), *indigenous innovation rates* were *strikingly high* in the U.S. (1.02), U.K. (0.76), and Finland (0.55) while indigenous innovation was strikingly *low* in Germany (0.42), Italy (0.40), and France (0.32). From the perspective of *Schumpeter's theory*, the latter nations must have had too few *entrepreneurs*. From the perspective of the *new, modern theory*, however, it can be seen as striking evidence of huge differences — even among G7 nations — in the dynamism of the *people* at work!

An analysis of data calculated by Gylfi Zoega shows that among people in the 20 OECD countries those possessing *high-strength doses* of the *modern values* — the U.S., Ireland, Australia, Denmark — less so Switzerland, Austria, U.K, Finland, and Italy — have relatively *high rates* of indigenous innovation, as the new theory of innovation predicts.[9] (Those with the least modern values — Japan, Norway, and Greece – had the lowest indigenous innovation.)

Another dimension of society's gain from having modern values is its job satisfaction. Zoega's analysis shows that the countries most endowed with the "right values" tended also to have the most job satisfaction.[10]

In another analysis, Bojilov shows the estimated time-path of "*Schumpeterian innovation*," 1890-2012, to be well below the estimated time-path of *indigenous innovation* in every one of the innovative nations of that time – the U.S., France and U.K, also Italy, and Germany.[11] On the whole, Schumpeterian innovation is *not* estimated to be at all important.

These four studies give telling evidence of the *existence and power* of a people's *dynamism* and an exciting test of the greater power of indigenous innovation over the power of exogenous innovation. The dynamism of the people won. The existing investigations of economic performance have attributed them to differences in institutions — thus paying little or no attention to values.[12]

These findings are hugely important. Where there is much dynamism, there is also an abundance of its fruits: achieving, succeeding, prospering, and flourishing! Where it is lacking, there is a joyless society.

Values are subject to change, however. The "modern values" that reached a critical mass in the 19th century (though initially articulated in much earlier epochs) were not strong enough at *first* to overcome other values, such as traditional ones like conformism, material rather than experiential goals, and fear of the unknown. Now it may be wondered whether some of the values that once fueled the dynamism in the West have *weakened* and whether some competing values have *strengthened*.

The Decline of Innovation and Its Causes — the Policy Section

With the roots of once-high innovation in the West understood, we can address the problem that arose by the 1970s: innovating had *diminished* severely — first in Germany, then Britain, later Italy, and lastly America and France. (Total factor productivity growth, which by historical standards had been rapid in the period 1950 – 1970 in America — Robert Gordon in his book locates this period as 1933-1972 — and extraordinarily rapid in France and Italy, fell to very slow rates in all four countries over the years 1970–1990, then *partially* recovered in America and Britain while *slowing further* in France and Italy.)[13] Now, in America and Germany, and especially France and Italy, the growth rates of total factor productivity since 2005 have fallen to grave levels.[14]

The *economic costs* to the West caused by the *loss* of innovation are serious. The resulting near-stagnation of wage rates is deeply disturbing to workers who had grown up believing that their wages would be rising enough to provide them a standard of living markedly better than they saw when growing up. As capital investments were running into "diminishing returns," no longer offset by impressive "technical progress," much capital formation has been discouraged. As real interest rates sunk to lower levels, the price of many assets, such as houses, rose inexorably from around 1973 to 2019, so fewer than ever can afford to live in them. (The post-Covid years still resemble that portrait, though new sources of uncertainty are changing things.)

The *social* costs are also serious. The loss of indigenous innovation may have brought a serious *decline* of the *meaningful work* that once engaged employees and brought them considerable *job satisfaction*. Those who had been engaged in the conception and development of new products and methods must have felt deprived of those deeply-felt rewards.

What are the causes of all this? Some observers, including adherents of the *neoclassical* school, might attribute the large loss of innovation to an unexplained fall-off in the rate at which scientists are making discoveries. Others who have stressed the importance of institutions, such as Daron Acemoglu, have argued that the corruption that has arisen in many corporations (and a few banks too) has surely weakened the interest that most firms in most industries had in innovating.[15] Still others, such as Thomas Philippon, have argued that the monopoly power of the new corporations arising with the new information technologies have been able to keep out any further start-ups.

In *Mass Flourishing*, I point to a rise in America of the corporatism that first arose in Hungary, Portugal, and Italy in the Interwar years — a term introduced by Mussolini meaning a national economic system in which the important corporations are largely directed by the state. Certainly, the sense in a company that a new venture might not have the support of the nation's leadership — that a Duce or Fuhrer who might be keen on guiding the economy in another direction — would dampen incentives to develop new concepts and discourage people from dreaming up new concepts.

However, I would argue that the decline of innovation (and thus the decline of its rewards) is attributable in large part to a *deterioration* of *key values* that fuel the dynamism of the people. There is much evidence of that deterioration. A chapter of *Mass Flourishing*, "Understanding the Post-1960s Decline," considers that the horrific rise of the "money culture," in John Dewey's term, may weaken a nation's dynamism."[16] Now, the later book *The Decadent Society* (2020) by Ross Douthat describes over a wide canvas the deterioration of the new character of Americans in recent years.[17]

But I sense now the problem is bigger than that. There may be a kind of "multiplier" at work. A contraction in the supply of modern values decreases the amount of economic growth supplied, and a demoralizing loss of growth may induce a further loss of values.

Although we do not have broad data on empirical *measures* of the decline in values that I have argued here are crucial to broad innovation conceived by large numbers in the population, it does appear that all or at any rate the bulk of values that are required for widespread innovating throughout society have declined appreciably since the brilliant years of the West's past.

Now Western societies, some more than others, are in a crisis. Data from the G.S.S. household survey show that reported job satisfaction in America has been on a downhill slide since 1972. Pew Research Center surveys from the early 1970s to recent years show a downward trend in the reported degree of life satisfaction. Anne Case and Angus Deaton in *Deaths of Despair* show data on the outbreak of despair in America linking it to economic developments there.[18] Now, dissatisfaction and despair are widespread.

We economists have not recognized that, for several decades, *people* want — people in the West at least — need *rich lives*. They need an economy in which jobs are *interesting, engaging* and occasionally *fun* too. A "good life" — a life of richness, as some humanists call it — means, for one thing, an occasional sense of *succeeding* — the feeling of *prospering* when your "ship comes in" or you gain recognition.[19] The good life *also* means a kind of *flourishing* — using one's imagination, exercising creativity, journeying into the unknown and acting on the world. A good economy holds out expectations of a good life. But a good life in much of society is more and more an *unmet* need. We may wonder whether key values can be restored without a change of society.

A new vision is required. I feel it may be necessary to *reconceive* the economy in which people devote their working lives. It is hugely important in my view that governments, both state and local, and thought-makers draw away from a focus bordering on obsession with *material gains*, hence a focus on income and wealth. The main business of this economy would be creating the new.

I envision an economy that is, in large part, a sprawling space with myriad studios for creating new things — an economy full of people in the business of creating things. In this new world, work is very engaging; and retiring from such work would be like retiring from life.

People need to realize their talents and aspirations! We economists ought to design an economy organized to enable people to have such working lives.

Endnotes

[1] See Edmund Phelps, *Mass Flourishing* (Princeton, NJ: Princeton University Press, 2013), also published in Chinese, French and Spanish; see also, Edmund Phelps with Raicho Bojilov, Hian Teck Hoon, and Gylfi Zoega *Dynamism: The Values that Drive Innovation, Job Satisfaction and Economic Growth* (Cambridge, MA: Harvard University Press, 2020).

[2] Paul Johnson, *The Birth of the Modern 1815-1830* (New York: Harper-Collins, 1991).

[3] F. W. Taussig, *The Tariff History of the United States* (New York and London: G.P. Putnam and Son, 1892), 57-58

[4] For centuries, Pico was one of two iconic figures at Oxford. He could be regarded the saint of creativity. (I was honored with the Premio Pico della Mirandola Award in 2008.)

[5] Abraham Lincoln, "Second Lecture on Discoveries and Inventions," Feb. 11, 1859.

[6] See *Mass Flourishing*, 1. See also Nicholas Conard, Maria Malina, and Susanne C. Münzel, "New Flutes Document the Earliest Musical Tradition in Southwestern Germany," *Nature,* August 2009, 737–740.

[7] See *Dynamism*, Fig. 2.5, p. 64, and Fig. 3.3, p. 72.

[8] See *Dynamism*, Table 2.1, p. 58.

[9] See *Dynamism*, Fig. 5.2, p. 117.

[10] See *Dynamism*, Figure 5.3, p. 118.

[11] See *Dynamism*, Fig. 2.3, p. 61.

[12] Douglass North, *Institutional Change and American Economic Growth* (Cambridge: Cambridge University Press, 1971).

[13] Robert Gordon, *The Rise and Fall of American Growth: The U.S. Standard of Living since the Civil War* (Princeton, NJ: Princeton University Press, 2016).

[14] There was *no revival* of the growth rate of total factor productivity following the "IT revolution," *i.e.* the emergence of "information technology," despite all the anecdotal evidence that comes from industry-and microlevel studies. See *Dynamism*, 68-84.

[15] Daron Acemoglu and James A. Robinson, *Why Nations Fail: The Origins of Power, Prosperity and Poverty* (New York: Currency, 2013). David Gelles, *The Man Who Broke Capitalism* (New York, Simon & Schuster, 2022).

[16] *Mass Flourishing*, 250.

[17] Ross Douthat, *The Decadent Society: How We Became Victims of Our Own Success* (New York: Simon and Schuster, 2020).

[18] Angus Deaton and Anne Case, *Deaths of Despair and the Future of Capitalism* (Princeton, NJ: Princeton University Press, 2021).

[19] See also David Ellwood and Nisha Patel, "Restoring the American Dream," Report to the Malcolm Wiener Center for Social Policy. Jan. 2018. Malcolm Wiener commented to me via email, "Economic success is...fundamental. But having a sense of agency and a say over the trajectory of your life, and being valued in community — belonging — are as important" (January 24, 2018).

Part II
How Policymakers Inhibit
or Promote Dynamism
in Our Economy

3. Dynamism and Stagnation: An Outlook

Edward Glaeser

The ability to be flexible, dynamic, and responsive is particularly important during moments of shock, when outside forces are roiling the economy and society. Unprecedented external shocks, from the pandemic to wars to whatever other enormous event is happening geopolitically, define our current moment. At the same time, reacting to shocks has become increasingly difficult, because we have hamstrung ourselves. Our world is constantly changing but we have not positioned ourselves to respond flexibly to that change.

For twenty years after the Second World War, Detroit chugged along reasonably well despite have a relatively stagnant car industry. This stagnation became much more catastrophic when the industry faced global competition and radically increased gas prices in the 1970s. America's regions have been experiencing shocks, including from China, long before the shocks of the last five years. Yet some regions have responded to those shocks far better than others, partially based on local flexibility and entrepreneurship. In our largest cities today, the office markets face particularly large shocks due to the shift to working from home. Finding an effective response to that is going to be enormously difficult: our zoning codes have created islands of skyscrapers dedicated to offices with no other interspersing functions. Regulated single purpose streetscapes make it particularly hard for cities to be flexible and reshape.

We need dynamism and the risk of stagnation is severe. This talk's patron saint is Mancur Olson, who forty years ago wrote *The Rise and Decline of Nations*. Here are two quotations:

> Stable societies with unchanged boundaries tend to accumulate more collusions and organizations for collective action over time.

Distributional coalitions slow down a society's capacity to adopt new technologies and to reallocate resources in response to changing conditions and thereby reduce the rate of economic growth.

In 1988, when I first read this book in graduate school, Olson's prediction sounded a bit like New York City or parts of California, but we had Texas and Ronald Reagan. American as a whole did not seem so sclerotic. Thirty-five years later, Olson's view increasingly describes America, not just pre-Thatcher England. This is the world that surrounds us, a world in which there are rules that constrain whether you can open a new business or build a new structure.

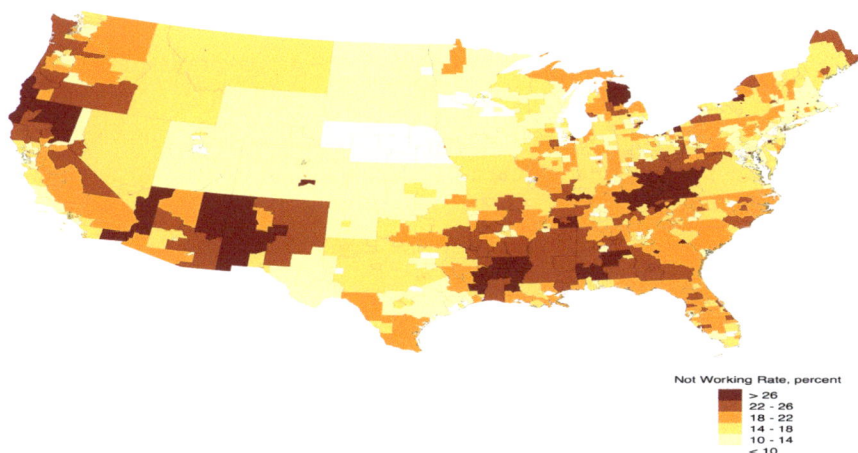

Geography of not working: Prime men 2015

Not Working Rate, percent
> 26
22 - 26
18 - 22
14 - 18
10 - 14
< 10

Responding to Economic Shocks

I am going to revisit territory that we already discussed at this year's Austin Symposium: America's incredible geographic disparities. This figure is from a paper I wrote with Larry Summers and Ben Austin. I believe that America's largest unsolved social problem is the rise of prime age joblessness, where the census defines prime age as between twenty-five and fifty-four. When I was born in 1967, roughly one in twenty prime age males were jobless. For most of the past fifteen years, more than fifteen percent of prime age males have been jobless. This is a big problem because every available piece of evidence shows that for men in particular, joblessness is vastly more catastrophic than being a low wage worker.

A job is not just about earnings: it is about purpose and social connection. The evidence shows that there are dangers associated with joblessness, including misery, suicide, and opioid abuse. Compared to being a low wage worker, joblessness appears to be catastrophic.

I differentiate between men and women, because women not formally in the labor force are still working by providing family care and incredible social value. I know you have seen articles on *The New York Times* website that praise the wonderful house husband, who is doing great work caretaking for his kids and parents. But the American Time Use Survey shows that jobless men have not increased their time in caring for others to any meaningful degree. They do, however, watch much more television. *The New York Times* has found an ideal, but it does not describe the norm for unemployed American men.

And male joblessness is not spatially neutral. There is a joblessness arc that courses through America's Eastern heartland. It begins down in Louisiana and Mississippi and runs up through Appalachia. It ends in the American Rust Belt, where often more than one in four prime age men is unemployed. This catastrophic situation reflects a failure to respond to different two shocks. First, these areas did not respond to the deindustrialization shock. (In some places, this is also the China shock.) The second shock is generous social benefits, including state level social benefits. Sometimes these men's girlfriends will bail them out or their parents will let them sleep on their couches. More than a third of prime age men are living in their parents' homes. There is an informal social safety net that accompanies the federal social welfare assistance and helps make this possible.

Growth in Inflation Corrected CPI Case-Shiller House Indices

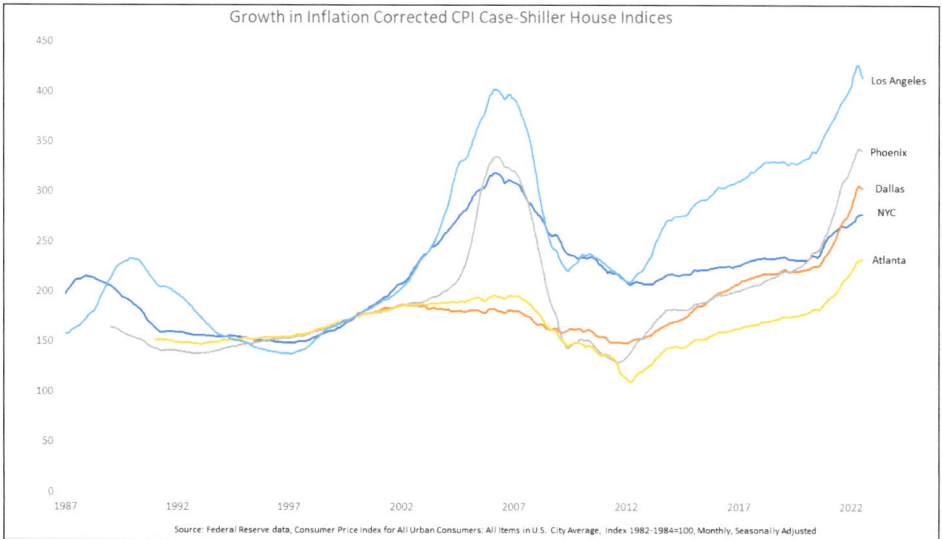

Source: Federal Reserve data, Consumer Price Index for All Urban Consumers: All Items in U.S. City Average, Index 1982-1984=100, Monthly, Seasonally Adjusted

These two shocks have led to joblessness. Two entrepreneurial failures have meant that our country has not been flexible enough in response to those shocks. One failure is that entrepreneurs have failed to create jobs for less skilled men who are not otherwise working in their home regions. The second failure is that builders have been unable to make enough space for them in the country's most productive areas. There are jobs in San Francisco, Los Angeles, and Atlanta, but these men are not moving to these productive places partially because the cost of living is too high.

The Rise of Associations that Block Building

Save the Bay in California: Suburban Environmentalists   Urban Preservationists in New York

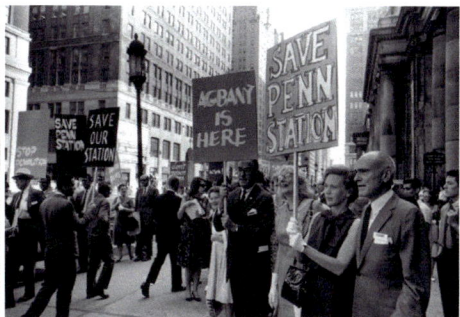

These are pictures of often sympathetic-seeming groups that figured out how to organize to block building in America. On the left are the pioneering leaders of the Save the Bay Foundation in greater San Francisco. One of these women is the wife of Berkeley's former Chancellor Clark Kerr. On the right are activists hoping to save Penn Station.

In America's lower density areas, the language of NIMBY-ism—not in my backyard-ism—is environmental. This NIMBY-ism continues even when not building is worse for the environment than building. My work with Matthew Kahn finds that carbon emissions are vastly lower in coastal California because of its innately moderate temperature. If we really wanted to lower America's carbon footprint, we would build energetically by the San Francisco Bay. But too many environmental activists have decided just to say no to building.

By contrast, NIMBY-ism in the urban core focuses on historic preservation. Regardless of how architecturally undistinguished a building is, someone will argue that it needs to be preserved, and the neighborhood needs to be protected from development. This provides the ideological cover for saying no to change. It is not obvious how much of this antipathy towards change is rational. Some people do not want their home prices to decrease, and others want to avoid the inconvenience of new people moving into the neighborhood. Some of it may be blind fear of the unknown.

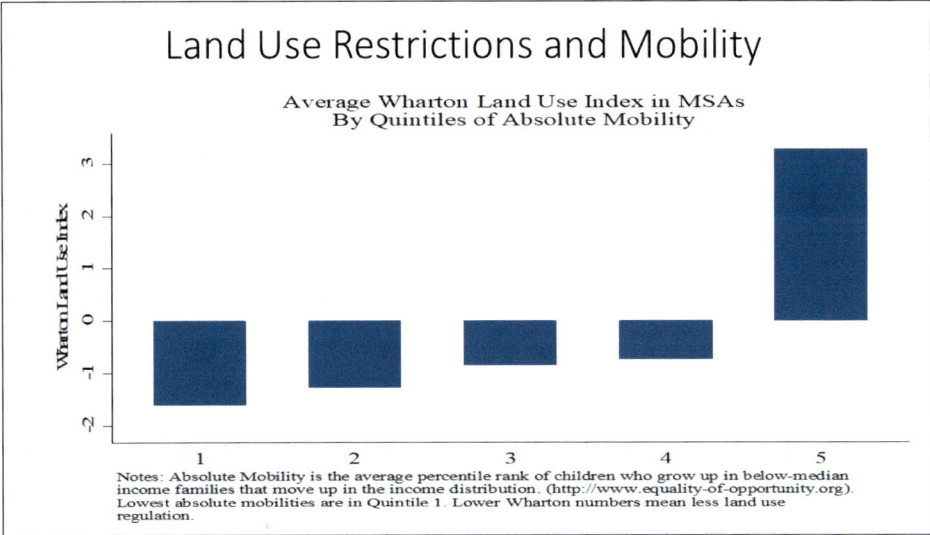

Land Use Restrictions and Mobility

Average Wharton Land Use Index in MSAs
By Quintiles of Absolute Mobility

Notes: Absolute Mobility is the average percentile rank of children who grow up in below-median income families that move up in the income distribution. (http://www.equality-of-opportunity.org). Lowest absolute mobilities are in Quintile 1. Lower Wharton numbers mean less land use regulation.

A crucial element is that highly educated people are particularly good at preventing building. Consequently, the barriers to growth are most severe in America's most educated areas. Those educated regions, however, would be the best places to build if you wanted to promote upward mobility. Along this figure's horizontal axis, I have ranked areas based on Raj Chetty's measure of how well poor children are rising into middle income adulthood. Along the vertical axis, I show how restrictive the building code is according to the Wharton Urban Land Use Survey. The areas that would offer the most upward mobility are also those that say no to building most often.

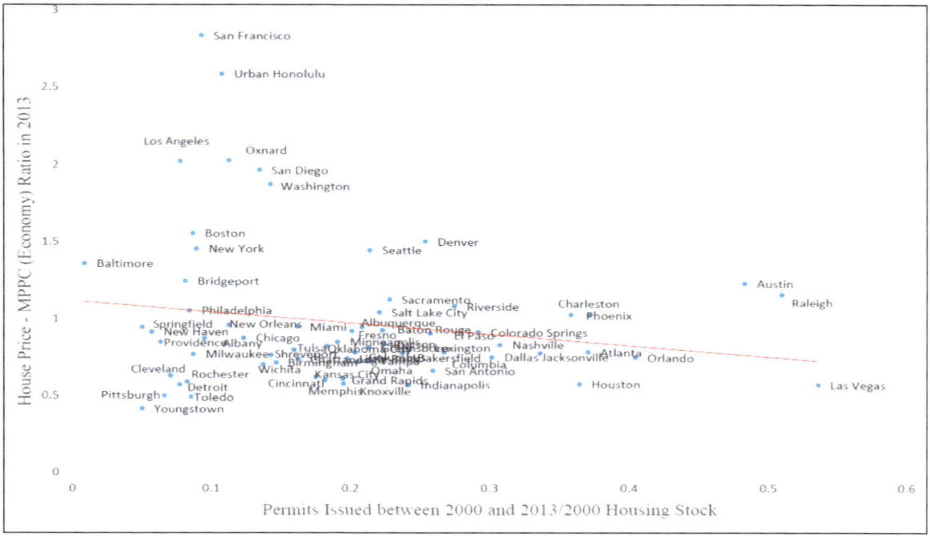

I now want to highlight how land use restrictions restrict American dynamism. I took this graph from a *Journal of Economic Perspectives* article that I wrote together with Joseph Gyourko. Along the horizontal axis is the amount of new construction permitted in the metropolitan area between 2000 and 2013 relative stock of housing in 2000. Along the vertical axis is the gap between how much it costs to buy a house and how much it costs to build a house. The number three, for example, shows that in Honolulu, buying a house is three times more expensive than building a house.

This graph shows that there is no way to repeal the laws of supply and demand. If demand for an area is robust, then this will either lead to more building, higher prices, or both. Making building very easy, like Austin has traditionally done, leads to wildly increasing population and moderate prices. Blue state Massachusetts may claim to care about affordable housing, but red state Texas actually provides vast more successfully affordable housing, just by unleashing private developers. There is plenty of demand to live in San Francisco and Los Angeles, but because it is so difficult to build there, that demand shows up in higher prices, not more homes.

The Slowdown in Construction Productivity (from joint work with Leo D'Amico, Joe Gyourko, Bill Kerr, and Giacomo Ponzetto)

In my past work on land use controls with Wharton's Joe Gyourko, we refer to the gap between building costs and purchasing costs as the "regulation tax." In our work, we found that about one-half of a New York City apartment's cost is due to regulation. That is the gap between how much it costs to add one more story to a building and how much that extra space is worth in the market. But what if regulations also shape the physical building costs? What if, over the long haul, we have created a building industry that is far less dynamic and productive than it could be because we have created these rules make it difficult to efficiently supply new housing?

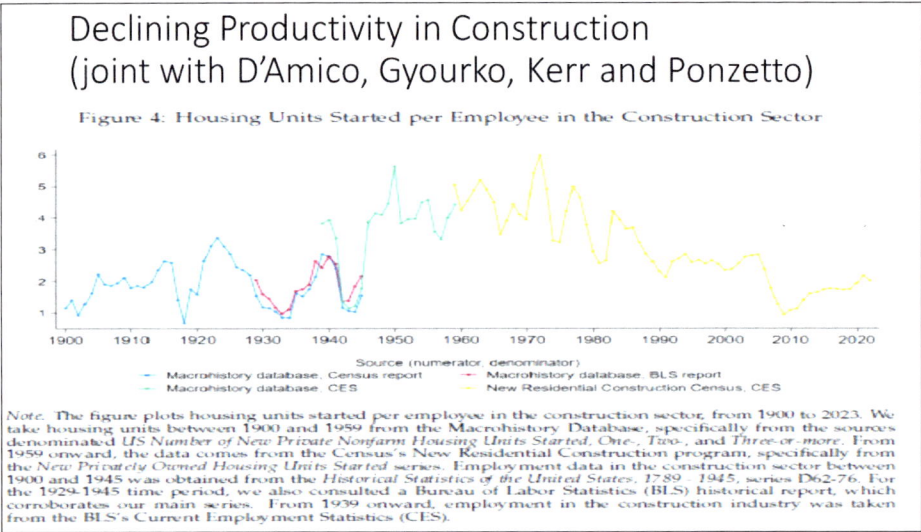

Declining Productivity in Construction
(joint with D'Amico, Gyourko, Kerr and Ponzetto)

Figure 4: Housing Units Started per Employee in the Construction Sector

Source (numerator, denominator)
- Macrohistory database, Census report   — Macrohistory database, BLS report
- Macrohistory database, CES   — New Residential Construction Census, CES

Note. The figure plots housing units started per employee in the construction sector, from 1900 to 2023. We take housing units between 1900 and 1959 from the Macrohistory Database, specifically from the sources denominated *US Number of New Private Nonfarm Housing Units Started, One-, Two-,* and *Three-or-more.* From 1959 onward, the data comes from the Census's New Residential Construction program, specifically from the *New Privately Owned Housing Units Started* series. Employment data in the construction sector between 1900 and 1945 was obtained from the *Historical Statistics of the United States, 1789 - 1945,* series D62-76. For the 1929-1945 time period, we also consulted a Bureau of Labor Statistics (BLS) historical report, which corroborates our main series. From 1939 onward, employment in the construction industry was taken from the BLS's Current Employment Statistics (CES).

This figure, which is from a working paper I jointly authored with Leo D'Amico, Joe Gyourko, Bill Kerr, and Giacomo Ponzetto, shows the ratio between housing units built and construction sector employees over the long haul. The graph shows that there is a period from 1940 where homes per worker remained relatively flat. Between the late 1940s and 1970, homes per worker soared. But since 1970, homes per worker has fallen, which echoes Austan Goolsbee and Chad Syverson's important work on productivity in the construction sector.

What happened? In the immediate post-war period, mass production made the construction sector more productive. The Levitts and other builders were copying Henry Ford and figuring out how to reap scale economies in housing production. They did not build the home in factories, but rather on site. Still, these builders figured out how to create something like an assembly line, where construction workers went up and down the street doing their bit for each house and then moving on. This enabled builders to supply the housing that returning American soldiers were eager to buy, especially with the help of thirty-year Veterans' Administration mortgages.

But starting in 1970, the projects start getting smaller. Communities get much better at saying no, and the available land parcels tended to shrink a bit. As the projects get smaller, the companies get smaller, and productivity decreased. Smaller companies invested less in R&D, and the whole industry stagnated. In our paper, we highlight the difference between regulation of entry, which means that you have a few dominant firms such as Detroit's big three in 1950, versus regulation of process, which means that instead of having big firms and big projects, you get small firms and small projects.

The next set of figures make the point that America's builders are tiny. The first figure shows the size of establishments that make single-family home construction and the size distribution of establishments in other core economic sectors. Most industries have most of their employment in establishments with more than 500 employees, but most workers in single-family residential construction are in establishments with fewer than ten workers. These are tiny firms. It is unreasonable to expect mom-and-pop operations to effectively build nearly all our single-family homes.

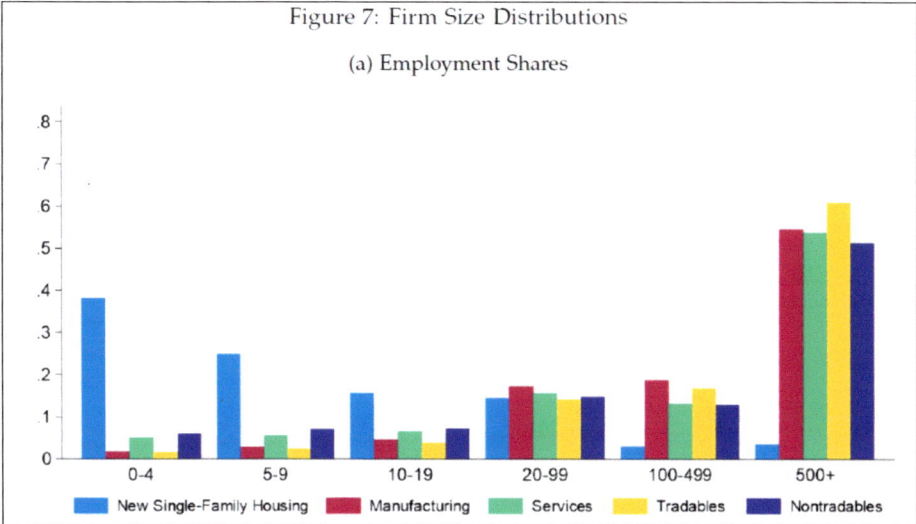

Figure 7: Firm Size Distributions

(a) Employment Shares

Legend: New Single-Family Housing, Manufacturing, Services, Tradables, Nontradables

The next figure is a map showing the size distribution of residential, single-family builders across American states. The dark blue states average more than 4.56 workers per establishment, which is the national average. In Texas, there are more than 4.5 workers per establishment, but all the lighter places have fewer than 4.5 workers on average in the median establishment. Those are tiny firms.

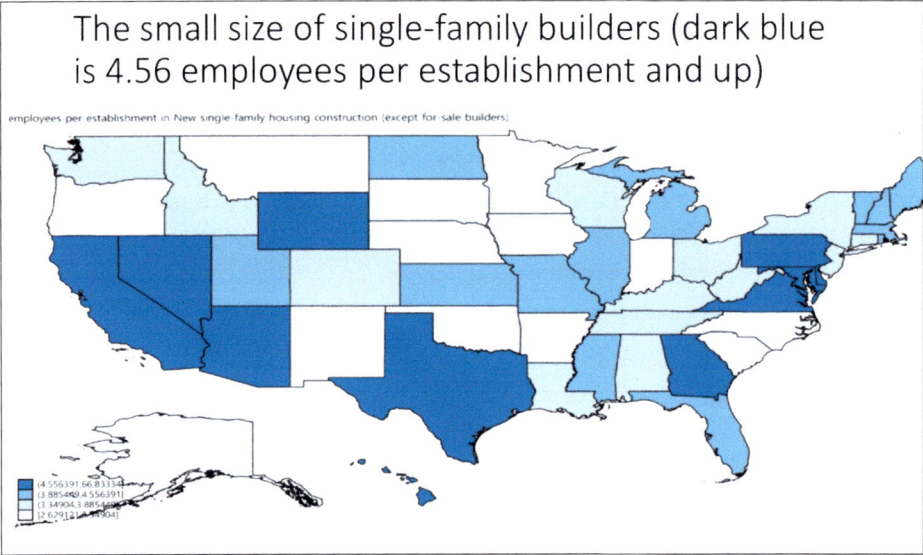

The small size of single-family builders (dark blue is 4.56 employees per establishment and up)

employees per establishment in New single-family housing construction (except for-sale builders)

(4.556391 66.83334)
(3.88549 4.556391)
(3.34904 3.88549)
(2.62912 3.34904)

The next table shows the correlation over space between one measure of regulation, the Wharton Residential Land Use Regulation Index (WRLURI). The top panel shows correlations with the actual WRLURI measure. The bottom panel shows correlations with a projected regulation index, which is formed by using demographics to predict the index where we have the index and then forming predicted values for a much larger range of metropolitan areas. All four columns tell a similar story: the most regulated areas have the least employment in large construction firms.

Table 7: Fraction of Employment in Large Firms and Regulation

VARIABLES	(1) All construction	(2) Construction of buildings	(3) Heavy and Civil Engineering	(4) Specialty Trade Contractors
Panel A: original WRLURI				
WRLURI	-0.0354***	-0.0607***	-0.0396*	-0.0328**
	(0.0128)	(0.0146)	(0.0217)	(0.0128)
ln of population (2008-2012)	0.0742***	0.0797***	0.1096***	0.0732***
	(0.0093)	(0.0092)	(0.0111)	(0.0081)
Constant	-0.5453*	-1.1150***	-0.8687*	-0.8772**
	(0.3213)	(0.3390)	(0.4436)	(0.3454)
Other controls	✓	✓	✓	✓
Observations	541	488	381	532
R-squared	.3639	.3251	.3382	.409
Panel B: projected WRLURI				
WRLURI	-0.0618***	-0.0795***	-0.0963**	-0.0332
	(0.0222)	(0.0268)	(0.0381)	(0.0225)
ln of population (2008-2012)	0.0756***	0.0801***	0.1145***	0.0721***
	(0.0086)	(0.0081)	(0.0098)	(0.0077)
Constant	-0.6836**	-1.1601***	-1.2885***	-0.7820**
	(0.2907)	(0.2943)	(0.4695)	(0.3384)
Other controls	✓	✓	✓	✓
Observations	846	730	541	830
R-squared	.3719	.3302	.3673	.4079

Higher housing regulation levels are associated with smaller firms. As a direct measure of innovation in construction, we look at patenting activity in the next figure.

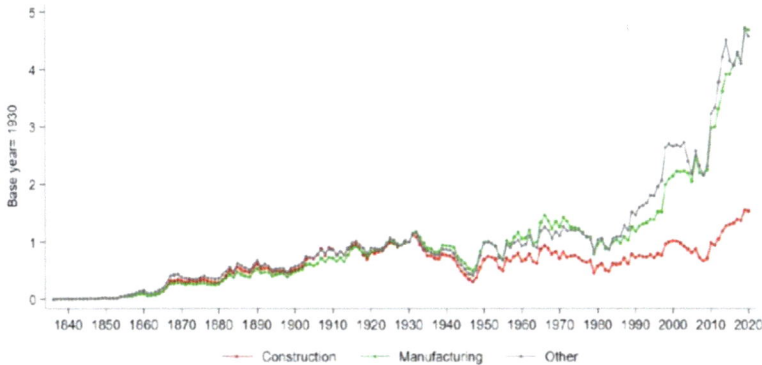

Figure 15: Patent levels by industry

Note. The figure plots by industry the relative patent levels over time for US-based inventors, with the series for the construction sector, the manufacturing sector, and other industries indexed to 1930.

The red line shows patenting in construction. The green line shows patenting in manufacturing and the gray line shows other industries. In all cases, we have indexed patenting levels so that all three series equal one in 1930. The three series track each other almost perfectly through the late 1940s. Between 1950 and 1970, a slight window opens, in which construction begins to lag. Then the series completely diverged after 1970, which is compatible with the view that construction became far less innovative after that time period.

Table 1: International Building Costs for a 20-Floor Office Building

	Total Cost	Labor Costs	Material Costs	Plant Costs	Unexplained Residual	WRLURI
	$/m^2$	$/m^2$	$/m^2$	$/m^2$	$/m^2$	
New York	6,994	3,037	1,500	1,645	813	1.05
San Francisco	6,540	3,100	1,219	1,535	686	1.22
Los Angeles	5,602	2,430	1,232	1,287	653	0.65
Chicago	4,642	1,985	1,275	1,316	67	−0.12
Houston	2,949	1,628	1,275	879	−834	−0.13
Paris	3,107	1,492	983	558	74	
Singapore	2,437	669	1,060	602	106	
Johannesburg	1,006	140	793	313	−241	
São Paulo	751	159	708	546	−662	
World Simple Average	3,004	1,182	1,137	706	−21	

Note. The table reports a decomposition of total building costs across labor costs, material costs, plant costs, and an unexplained residual as described in Equation (1). All costs are expressed in dollars per square meter. The last column adds, for the US cities in the sample, a measure of land-use regulatory tightness from Gyourko, Hartley, and Krimmel (2019).

As a final look at U.S. construction productivity, this table uses data from the company Turner and Townsend and compares the costs of building in different U.S. cities and a few comparison places. This data is meant to reflect the physical cost of building a twenty-story office building in different regions of the world. There is a big gap between less regulated Houston, where pure physical construction costs are cheaper, and more regulated San Francisco or New York. Our costs are also higher than our global comparison cities. One reason why America is less dynamic, is that we have gotten much worse at building structures and infrastructures. Regulatory sludge bears some blame for this, but our desire to ensure no one is ever inconvenienced is also a partial cause. We blanket the builders and procurement agents with rules, which makes it difficult to be nimble and innovative.

Responding to Disease-Related Shocks

Let us turn to our ability to respond to disease-related shocks, like the COVID-19 pandemic that hit the world in 2020. Cities have been enduring pandemics for thousands of years. Our first well documented urban pandemic is the Plague of Athens which began in 430 B.C. Fifth-century Athens was doing everything you could imagine wanting a city to do. A genius stood on every street corner. Euripides, Aeschylus, and Sophocles were writing dramatic plays that still resonate with us today. Phidias was revolutionizing sculpture. Herodotus and Thucydides, the two fathers of history, lived and worked there. Democracy itself was being born and on top of that, Athens was an economic and military powerhouse.

All this success excited the envy of Athens' land based, non-urban, highly militarily successful rival: Sparta. Sparta demanded that Athens stand down from its leadership of the Delian League. In his famous Funeral Oration, a speech that would have made Sam Houston himself proud, Pericles tells the Spartans that he would take guff from no man, and that kickstarted the Peloponnesian War.

Pericles' plan was to summon the Athenians and their Attic allies behind Athens' walls, trusting those walls to keep out the superior Spartan army. Then he would send the vastly superior Athenian fleet to harass the Peloponnese coastline. As military strategy, it worked perfectly well: the walls held against the hoplites. But walls that can keep out enemy warriors may not manage to keep out a virus or bacteria.

Cities are vulnerable to pandemics for two reasons. First, they are the nodes on our global travel and trade lattice; they are the entry ports for goods, people, ideas, and viruses. It was so in New York City in 2020 and its was so with the Athenian port of Piraeus in 430 B.C. Something entered the city, probably from Asia, and started laying waste.

Cities' second vulnerability is the proximity of its inhabitants. People living close together can often be an asset, but it also enables easy travel for bacteria and viruses. Thucydides described a city that had run amok, in which people live only for the day, because they expect to die tomorrow. The plague caused the deaths of around twenty-five percent of Athens' population, a death rate one hundred times that of COVID-19. Athens' greatness allowed it to keep fighting the Peloponnesian War for another twenty-three years before losing, but in some sense the plague dimmed its luster forever. When Athens emerged from the war, it slipped from being the New York City of the eastern Mediterranean to the Philadelphia, and then the New Haven.

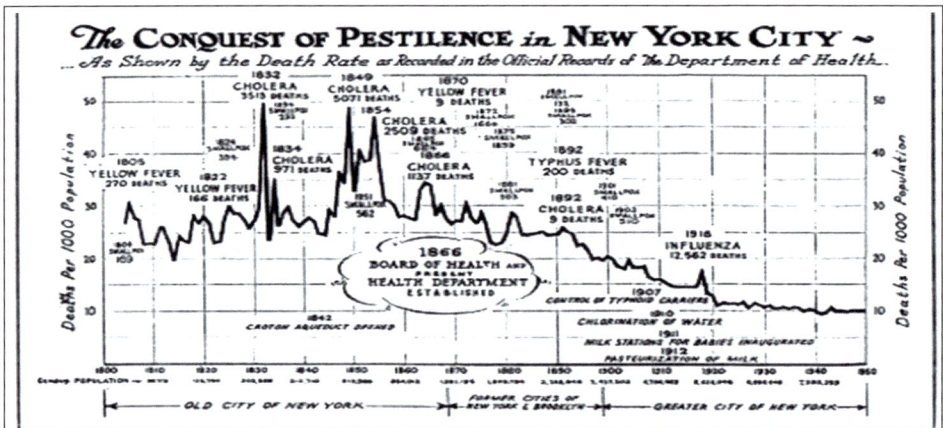

New York City's Department of Health shows the timeline of the city's mortality rate, which sharply dropped with the provision of clean water in the nineteenth century.

New York City Department of Health and Mental Hygiene

Over much of the past 650 years, our cities have been relatively resilient to pandemic. This figure shows the path of New York City's death rates over the last two hundred years. The early 19th century was a period of proto-globalization and proto-globalization meant proto-plague. The early decades of the 19th century experienced yellow fever, a mosquito borne illness that emerged out of Africa in the late 17th century. Sailing ships carried it along to the Caribbean and from there it moved north to East Coast cities. Yellow fever's death rate was two and a half percent, making it ten times more fatal than COVID-19 and one-tenth as fatal as the Plague of Athens.

Another plague was a particularly virulent strand of Cholera, which emerged in the Ganges Delta in 1817. The British Army carried it over the sea and from there it made its way to North American ports. Cholera's death rates reached almost five percent.

But despite these death levels, cities continued to grow. They were just that productive. If your alternative to living in a city was dying of starvation in Ireland, facing the plague risk in New York might not be too bad. Cities also continued to grow because their governments started investing in infrastructure that mattered. In *Survival of the City*, David Cutler and I highlight this as a hinge of history. This is the point at which governments started doing something other than killing people. Eighteenth century and earlier Western governments were basically in the death business.

As much as we may celebrate Frederick the Great and Voltaire's eloquent correspondence or his patronage of the mathematician Lagrange, we must remember that Frederick the Great's day job was waging war and stealing Silesia from the Empress Maria Theresa. But starting in the 19th century, city governments suddenly started investing in clean water, sewers, and other infrastructure improvements that save lives. As a Chicago Ph.D., I am predisposed to the view that there are many things that governments should not do, like overregulate building or entrepreneurship, but there are certainly things that governments should do. Reducing the risk that your citizens will die of Cholera seems like a reasonable task for governments to undertake.

The health-related investments of the nineteenth century were functional. The were the product of a bottom-up movement, in which leading citizens built coalitions to support infrastructure improvements. Bond markets made it possible for cities to borrow enough to make these investments. Another theme of this talk is that we want our governments to make our roads smoother, to effectively defend America, and to improve our education systems, although I am certainly open to vouchers and charter schools. As a result of these 19th century investments in clean water and sewers, cities' health improved. Indeed, our cities became so much healthier between 1919 and 2019 that we almost forgot that cities could be killing fields. Then we suffered another plague.

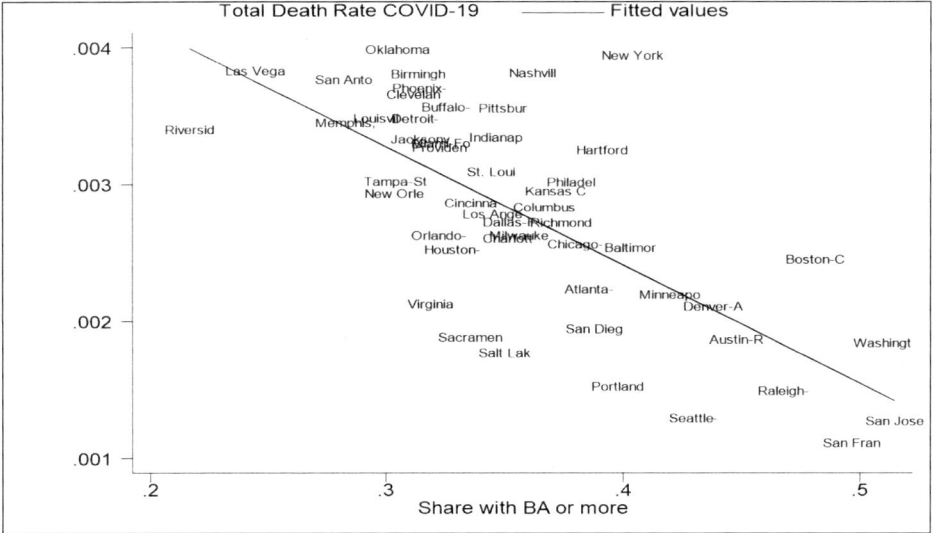

What is going to protect us against 21st century pandemic? Amazingly, education seems to be as protective against illness as it was earlier against the deindustrialization shocks of the 1960s and 1970s. This figure shows the relationship between total COVID death rates from 2020 to 2023 and the share of the adult population with a college degree. The amazing thing is not that there are fewer deaths in more educated metropolitan areas, but that the slope is so extreme: there is a four-fold difference among cities like Las Vegas, San Antonio and Oklahoma, where roughly four-tenths of one percent of the population died, to cities like San Jose and San Francisco where one-tenth of one percent of the population died. More people died in Seattle of fentanyl overdoses during the COVID pandemic than died of COVID.

This negative relationship also reflects the fact that more educated cities had the most extreme work from home practices and policies, which may have saved some lives, but also created an economic hangover. The education gap in working from home is enormous. In May 2020, during the pandemic, 68.9 percent of Americans with advanced degrees were working remotely while only five percent of high school dropouts were working remotely. What downtowns are still the most underused today? The hyper-educated metropolises, like San Francisco and Seattle.

The Gigantic Office Shock

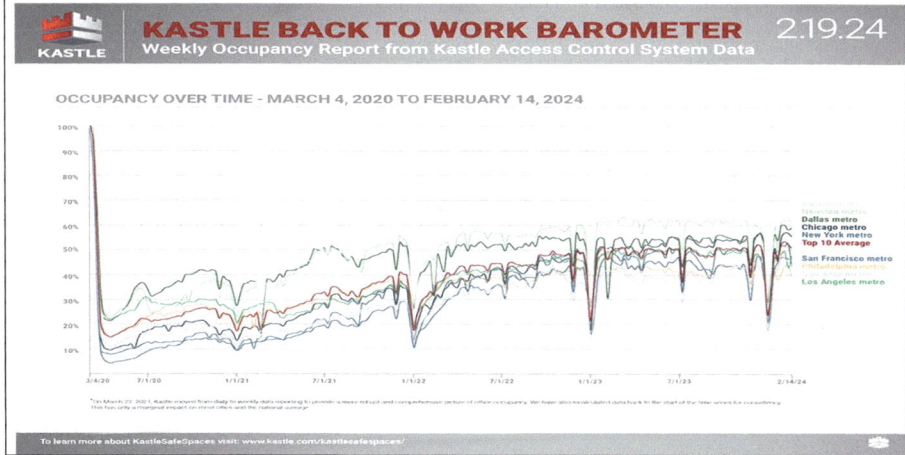

This figure shows data from Kastle Technologies from February, 2024. This measure of office vacancy is based on key swipes for people entering large office buildings. These fancy downtown offices are still at about fifty percent occupancy relative to pre-pandemic. Nationally, work from home is a much smaller phenomenon. About ten percent of workers nationwide are permanently work from home and around twelve percent are partially work from home.

Cities will manage to respond to the office vacancy shock only if they are flexible enough to change. This is not the first time America's cities have been under stress. In the 1970s, all of America's older, colder cities were heading to history's trash heap because of massive changes in transportation technology. Transportation costs shaped the destinies of all America's older cities. Each of the twenty largest U.S. cities in 1900 was on a major waterway. The oldest—New York and Boston—were built where the river meets the sea. Minneapolis, the newest, was built at the northernmost navigable point on the Mississippi River. These cities grew up as nodes on this great transportation network, but over the course of the twentieth century, transportation costs plummeted.

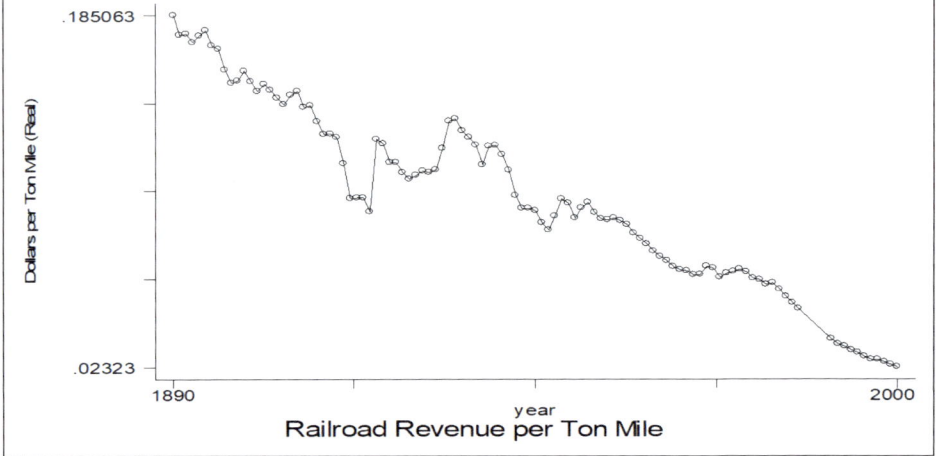

The Decline of the Costs of Moving Goods

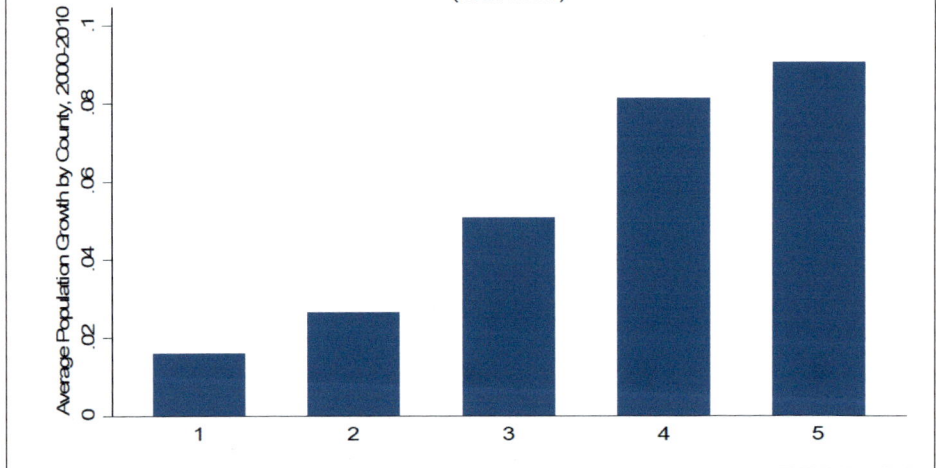

Average Population Growth by Average January Temperature (Quintiles)

The inflation-adjusted cost of moving a ton per mile by rail fell by ninety percent between 1890 and 2000. Container ships, the highway system, and air freight were causing even more amazing things to happen. Detroit's location with great waterways, railroads and proximity to America's agricultural heartland was a huge bonus in 1910 when Henry Ford started modern manufacturing. By 1960, however, Detroit was just a really cold place. Americans relocated.

January temperature is the best predictor of twentieth century metropolitan area growth for several reasons. Warmer places are more likely to be right-to-work states and they attracted industry after World War II. Tom Holmes's work found counties on the right-to-work sides of state borders experienced large increases in industrial employment after 1947 relative to neighboring counties in pro-union states. Warmer places have also made it much easier to build. But let's face it: Americans don't like driving on the ice for three months out of the year. As a New England parent who raised three kids amidst all that ice, that it shows a lack of character on America's part not to like those icy roads.

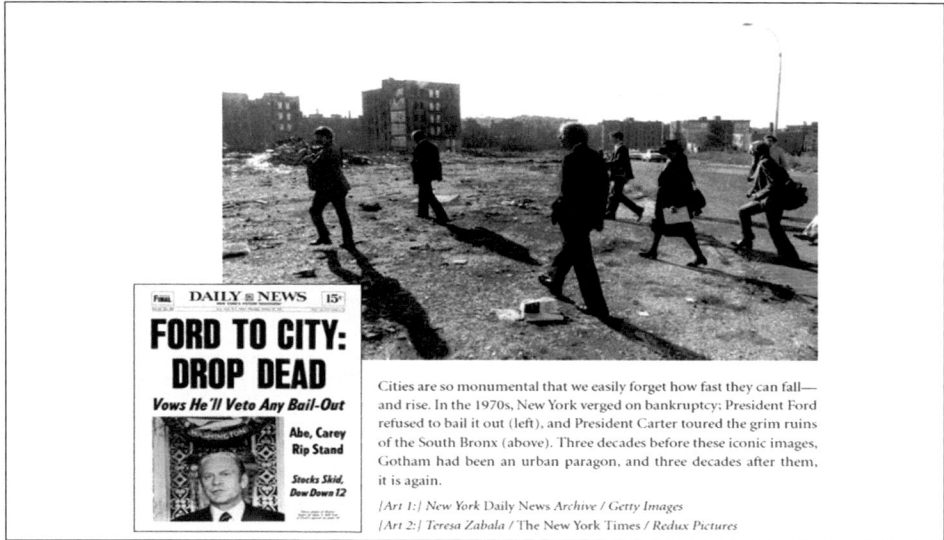

Cities are so monumental that we easily forget how fast they can fall— and rise. In the 1970s, New York verged on bankruptcy; President Ford refused to bail it out (left), and President Carter toured the grim ruins of the South Bronx (above). Three decades before these iconic images, Gotham had been an urban paragon, and three decades after them, it is again.

[Art 1:] *New York Daily News Archive / Getty Images*
[Art 2:] *Teresa Zabala / The New York Times / Redux Pictures*

These are iconic images from my youth. This is President Ford in New York during the 1970s fiscal crisis. It reflects that in addition to deindustrialization, crime had gone crazy. Fiscal responsibility was completely lacking. President Ford quite understandably refused to bail the city out and it really looked as if it was heading for catastrophe. The other photo is Jimmy Carter wandering through the wasteland South Bronx had become. The city looked doomed.

In 1971, two jokers put up a billboard on the highway leaving Seattle, asking the last person to leave to please turn off the lights. Just as no one could imagine Detroit with a smaller General Motors, no one could imagine Seattle with a smaller Boeing, and Boeing had been cutting back on jobs. But Seattle recovered, and urban density came back.

In 1980, Alvin Toffler, the hip futurist of his age, wrote a book predicting that all this fancy information technology—fax machines, personal computers—would make urban offices just as obsolete as containerships had made New York's garment district decades earlier. He looked forward to a world in which we would have empty skyscrapers that we would have to occupy as warehouses. His arguments were similar to what we have heard in today's urban doom loop literature.

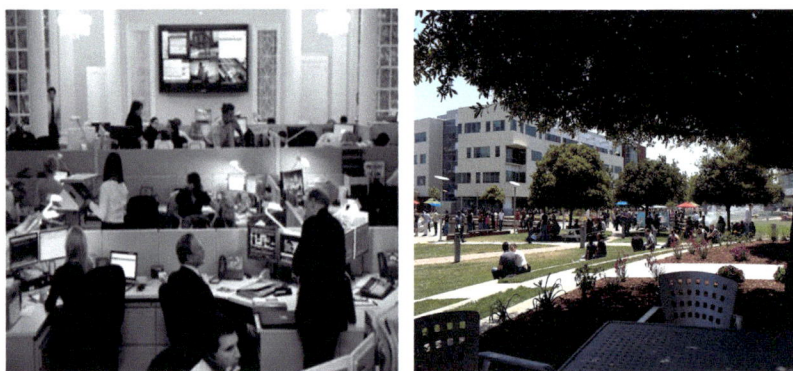

But urban density came back

Image by Runner1928

That did not happen, and instead, some American regions experienced an urban renaissance. The global economy's tidal forces came to favor face-to-face contact. There has been a vast rise in the return to skills and innovation. As a social species, we get smarter when we live and work around other smart people. If you do not know that face-to-face contact is incredibly valuable for learning, then you are not taking advantage of UT Austin. Our universities are designed to be machines for collaborative learning and innovation. Globalization adds to this by radically increasing the returns to innovation, partially because any great idea can be sold or built anywhere on the planet.

The left image is the wall-less office at Mike Bloomberg's City Hall, which is based on the wall-less office at Bloomberg L.P., which is based on the Salomon Brothers trading floor. Jamie Dimon was eager to bring trading floors back during the pandemic, and trading floors provide a great example of why face-to-face contact is so valuable: a little bit of extra information can make you a fortune in minutes on a trading floor. Finance is all about knowing what is going to happen. Traders learn a great deal amid the action. Neither COVID nor Zoom changed that fact. If information technology were making face-to-face contact obsolete, then why would Google buy the Googleplex? Why would they buy millions of square feet in downtown Manhattan if they did not think it was important to have young workers working together and learning from each other?

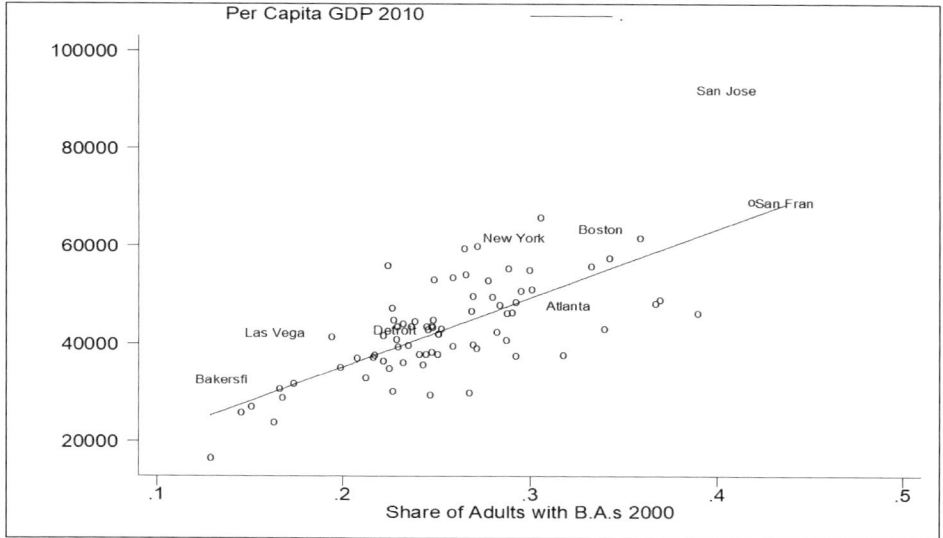

These benefits of face-to-face interaction did not enable Detroit, Cleveland, or many of the older, colder cities to recover from deindustrialization. They never reinvented themselves in the 1970s. If a city does not have Texas's pro-business environment and sunshine, it at least needs to have skills. This figure shows the relationship between share of the population with a B.A. and earnings. As the work of Jim Rauch and Enrico Moretti shows, the place-level connection between skills and economic success does not just reflect the fact that your skills make you more productive, it also reflects the fact that your neighbors' skills make you more productive. Economists call this phenomena "human capital externalities."

Typical estimates are that as the share of adults in your metropolitan area with a college degree goes up by ten percentage points, your earnings also go up by ten percentage points, holding years of schooling constant. If you live in highly skilled environments, then chances are that your neighbors have taught you something smart, or helped you find a job, or bought something from you. Having skilled people around you is valuable.

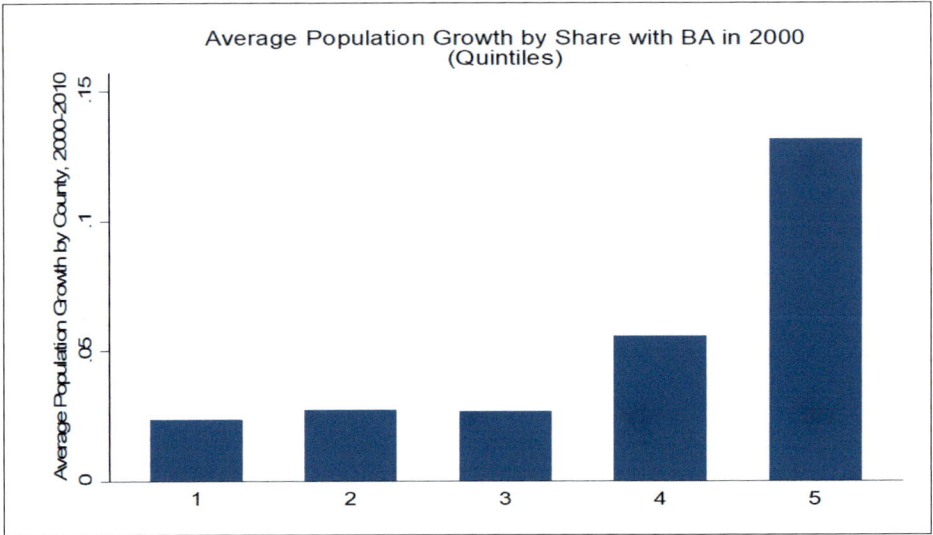

Average Population Growth by Share with BA in 2000 (Quintiles)

This shows that population growth has concentrated in highly skilled areas. The shift towards skilled areas has been particularly important in the colder northern parts of the country. The skills that matter are not necessarily the skills that schools teach; we tend to focus on those skills because they are measurable. In some sense, the most important skills for urban regenerations are those talents that relate to running a business, producing new innovations, and being functional in the world. Our colleges do not necessarily teach those.

Sixty years ago, economist Benjamin Chinitz compared New York and Pittsburgh and noted that New York appeared to be more resilient than Pittsburgh even then. This was because, he argued, New York had an entrepreneurship culture that had been inculcated in the city's massive garment industry. The garment sector was the U.S.'s largest industrial cluster in 1950s, significantly larger than Detroit's automobile industry. Moreover, garment production was unlike automobile production because there were no barriers to entry and very weak scale economies. Consequently, anyone with an innovative idea and a couple of sewing machines could start a business, and the garment industry became a school for entrepreneurs.

These entrepreneurs were flexible; they would start with garments and then start a movie studio, or build skyscrapers, or they would open a bank, because that's how entrepreneurial human capital works. It created a place that was flexible when shocked, which is of course this talk's fundamental theme. Even though New York City had a government that was dumping regulatory sludge on everyone, it had human capital that was maximally adaptive, which is what enabled it to change. Today's question is whether New York still retains that spirit sixty years later.

Economic Growth and Firm Size
MSA Employment Growth (1977-2010)
by Average Firm Size (1977) Quintiles

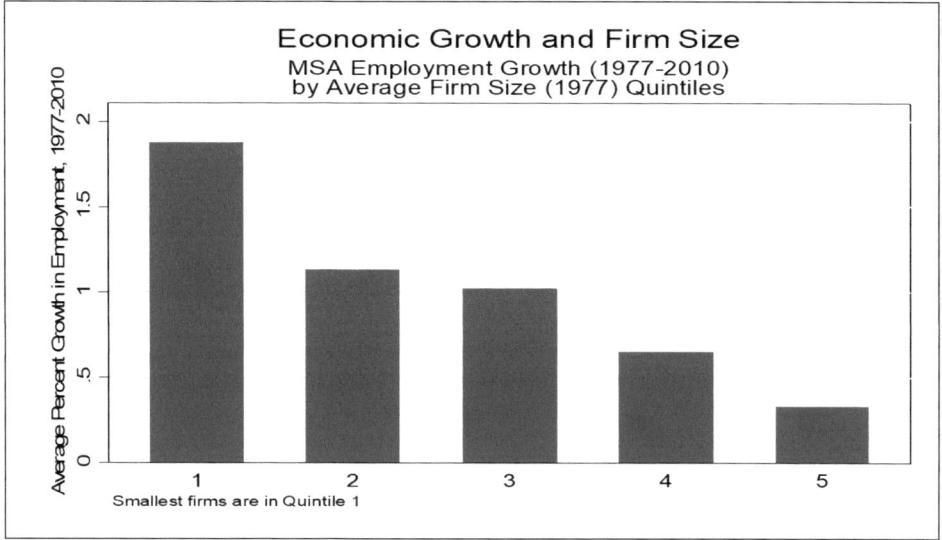

It is remarkable, given how mediocre our measures of entrepreneurial human capital are, that they predict urban growth so well. Economists use two measures of entrepreneurial human capital: average establishment size in an initial year and the share of employment in new establishments. Both are enormously predictive of which cities managed to have employment growth over the next thirty-three years. There is a fourfold difference between the places with the biggest establishments and the places with the smallest establishments. In past papers, I have documented that this is not just a result of industry choice or regional choice, but it reflects a real tendency of places with lots of nimble firms to add employment more quickly.

My prognosis is that Zoom is not going to mean an end to face-to-face contact, but it certainly does mean a more competitive talent environment. Imagine a hypothetical San Jose-based fifteen-person startup. I do not think a single employee would say "since we can Zoom, we should never bother to meet in-person again. We'll go to our parents' houses and save on housing costs." What seems more likely to me is that some employees would decide they want to live in Austin to avoid paying state taxes and still be around skilled people. Some would move to Vail because they like skiing or some to Honolulu because they like surfing. The market for talent has never been hotter. This is what our local governments face: an environment where they need to figure out how to get physical or regulatory systems that were designed for a different world to adapt to this new, highly competitive setting.

Measuring Urban Winners and Losers

- Earnings and employment data from the Quarterly Census of Employment and Wages goes to Third Quarter 2021
- Repeat home sales data from the Federal Housing Finance Agency (FHFA) from December 2021.
- Permit data from the Census of Construction covers the entire year 2021.
- Strategy is always to take percent changes over two year period.
- For the nominal variables (prices and earnings) we correct for inflation (CPI)– 7% from Q3 2019 to Q3 2021.
- The data are interesting on their own, but we also produce an index.

So which cities managed to do this well? We start the second edition of *Survival of the City* by measuring which cities did well and which did poorly. We chose four measures, primarily because of their relatively high frequency: changes in earnings and employment, which is coming from the quarterly census of employment wages; repeat home sales prices, from the FHFA repeat sales index; and permit data, meaning how much new construction is happening, including quantity of permits, prices, and quantity of employment wages. Then we divided these factors by the standard deviation of those factors across areas and created a z-score. And then we just took a simple arithmetic average of those four series.

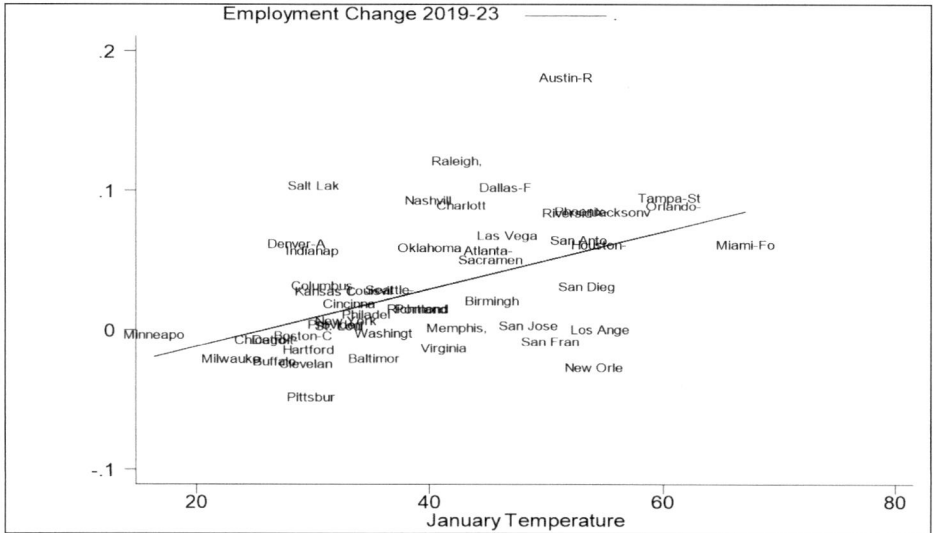
Employment Change 2019-23

What are the patterns? January temperature is predictive of positive outcomes, like employment change. We expected this because people want to be in safe, warm areas where they can spend time outside. Places with higher January temperatures also had fewer lockdown rules and enough people probably valued that too.

But these arguments cannot explain the positive relationship between January temperature and earnings growth the next figure shows.

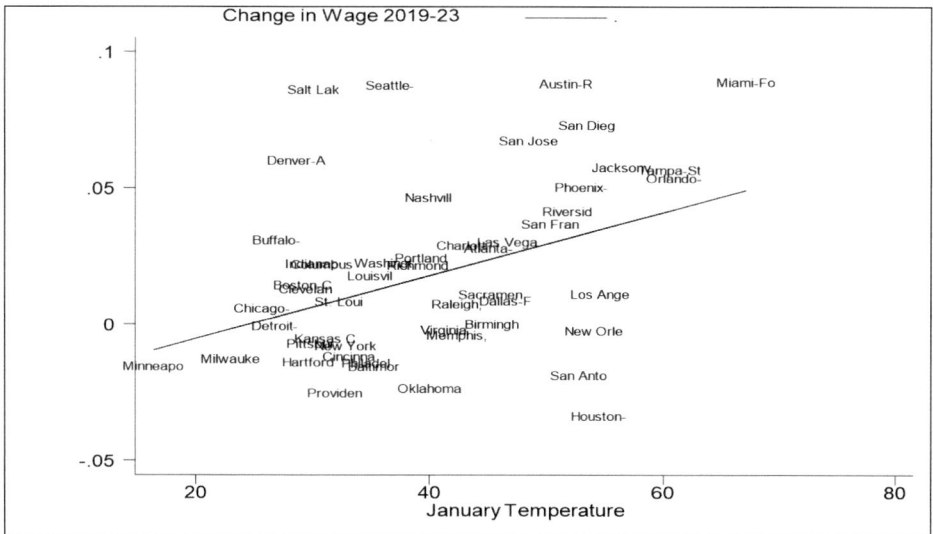
Change in Wage 2019-23

If people just want to live in warm areas, then the number of people moving to an area should be going up, but wages should be going down. A labor supply shift caused by attractive amenities is supposed to cause populations to rise and earnings to fall. But the fact that wages are going up is telling you this is not just about wanting to live in warmer places: firms also want to produce in warmer places. Warmer parts of America seem to have proven to be more dynamic and more adaptable in both the labor demand side and the supply side.

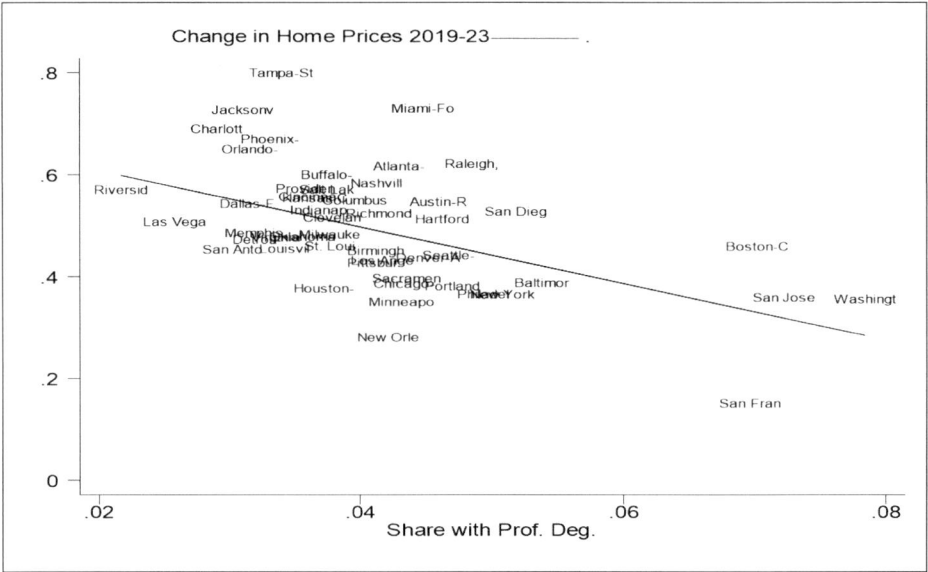

For most of the past forty years, skills have strongly positive predicted housing price growth. Over the COVID period, however, the opposite is true, perhaps precisely because of the link between skills and adaptability. Skilled workers have used Zoom to move away from expensive places like San Francisco, San Jose, Boston, and Washington D.C. Skilled workers have also experienced the largest shifts to work from home, which may make them less willing to pay for real estate that is close to their jobs.

Metropolitan Area	Percent Employment Growth	Percentage Weekly Wage Growth	Percentage Home Price Growth	Percent Change in Housing Permits
Austin-Round Rock-Georgetown, TX	14.12	5.67	32.95	24.29
Miami-Fort Lauderdale-Pompano Beach, FL	3.33	6.89	41.93	26.43
Tampa-St. Petersburg-Clearwater, FL	5.79	3.76	48.54	8.36
Salt Lake City, UT	7.81	2.84	32.79	57.15
Jacksonville, FL	5.97	3.01	39.70	42.16
Phoenix-Mesa-Chandler, AZ	5.23	2.03	41.08	48.21
Charlotte-Concord-Gastonia, NC-SC	5.47	2.55	40.38	34.53
Raleigh-Cary, NC	8.45	-3.04	34.90	97.66
Orlando-Kissimmee-Sanford, FL	5.46	3.08	34.68	14.01
Riverside-San Bernardino-Ontario, CA	7.42	0.69	29.00	49.35
Nashville-Davidson--Murfreesboro--Franklin, TN	6.02	1.24	34.56	29.53
San Diego-Chula Vista-Carlsbad, CA	1.66	2.59	27.24	42.88
Atlanta-Sandy Springs-Alpharetta, GA	3.53	0.32	34.06	25.47
Indianapolis-Carmel-Anderson, IN	3.82	0.62	28.49	36.98
Pittsburgh, PA	-5.57	-1.10	16.85	211.78
Dallas-Fort Worth-Arlington, TX	7.39	-0.81	28.50	3.58
San Antonio-New Braunfels, TX	4.22	0.33	23.97	32.46
Columbus, OH	1.09	-0.72	27.66	62.91
Denver-Aurora-Lakewood, CO	3.13	2.50	19.65	15.22
Sacramento-Roseville-Folsom, CA	3.14	0.62	15.48	55.89
Richmond, VA	0.14	0.21	27.95	27.57
Las Vegas-Henderson-Paradise, NV	4.03	0.69	21.73	1.53
Memphis, TN-MS-AR	0.76	1.00	31.50	-10.07
Virginia Beach-Norfolk-Newport News, VA-NC	-1.67	1.08	21.48	49.49
Providence-Warwick, RI-MA	-1.14	0.65	28.94	18.94

Metropolitan Area	Percent Employment Growth	Percentage Weekly Wage Growth	Percentage Home Price Growth	Percent Change in Housing Permits
Cincinnati, OH-KY-IN	0.60	-2.91	29.19	63.18
Louisville-Jefferson County, KY-IN	1.40	0.25	20.14	21.02
Seattle-Tacoma-Bellevue, WA	1.27	1.83	17.94	-12.40
Birmingham-Hoover, AL	1.02	-0.95	22.88	11.39
Buffalo-Cheektowaga, NY	-4.97	2.68	25.75	-7.48
Baltimore-Columbia-Towson, MD	-3.10	0.37	12.74	64.34
Boston-Cambridge-Newton, MA-NH	-1.53	0.07	18.28	25.81
Portland-Vancouver-Hillsboro, OR-WA	0.02	2.58	14.35	-24.60
St. Louis, MO-IL	-1.95	-1.16	19.46	26.99
Kansas City, MO-KS	0.71	-0.19	26.49	-58.36
Los Angeles-Long Beach-Anaheim, CA	-0.25	-0.64	17.36	-2.64
Cleveland-Elyria, OH	-3.51	0.68	23.67	-19.94
Milwaukee-Waukesha, WI	-3.02	-0.18	24.76	-24.87
Detroit-Warren-Dearborn, MI	-2.73	-1.37	20.97	-1.35
Chicago-Naperville-Elgin, IL-IN-WI	-1.97	-0.79	12.32	12.42
San Jose-Sunnyvale-Santa Clara, CA	0.43	0.71	9.64	-37.22
Houston-The Woodlands-Sugar Land, TX	2.96	-5.13	15.90	15.11
Oklahoma City, OK	2.84	-4.01	20.94	-29.46
Minneapolis-St. Paul-Bloomington, MN-WI	-2.18	-0.09	12.27	-14.14
New York-Newark-Jersey City, NY-NJ-PA	-1.90	-1.32	12.68	-2.73
New Orleans-Metairie, LA	-3.52	0.26	8.74	-1.03
Philadelphia-Camden-Wilmington, PA-NJ-DE-MD	-0.69	-1.91	12.07	-11.31
Hartford-East Hartford-Middletown, CT	-2.86	-4.28	22.52	-21.56
Washington-Arlington-Alexandria, DC-VA-MD-WV	-1.26	-2.93	11.83	-20.11
San Francisco-Oakland-Berkeley, CA	-1.12	2.99	-6.45	-56.94

Austin is the cover image on the hardcover edition of our book. Our editor did not choose it because he knew the numbers, but because he just knew that special things were happening here. Austin is so remarkable because it combines tremendous human capital with Texas's relatively pro-business environment. Those two factors make it a Sun Belt superstar.

When we put together our entire index, Austin ranked first by a considerable margin. One reason that Austin is so high on this chart because of incredible housing price growth. This will probably mean-revert at some point in time because it's relatively easy to build here. But changing housing permits way up relative to robust employment growth shows that most of the top twenty-five cities are in the Sun Belt.

The Sun Belt superstars completely dominate the top twenty-five. There are a lot of Rust Belt cities on the bottom twenty-five, but the real bottom are places that you wouldn't normally think of as being catastrophes: New York, for example, is down there. For most of the past forty years, New York has been soaring over most of the Rust Belt because its vast office market was an asset, rather than a curse. Now that vast, almost segregated office market has become a curse, in part because it takes people so long to get to work.

Washington D.C. is another example. Government is a stable employer, but for the last three years, it has been catastrophic for the city. I suspect the Federal government has fairly generous work from home policies. For many government agencies there's little competitive pressure to get people to show up. Of course, San Francisco is on the absolute bottom.

How can local governments respond to this dynamic and become flexible? In a world where talent is mobile, you need to provide an environment where people want to live. This is the idea of the consumer city: you want to attract people to vibrant downtowns. Government's job is not to micromanage industrial growth; it is to attract and train smart people and then get out of their way. That is not laissez-faire, because attracting and training smart people requires public safety, the management of city streets, and other core public services.

One of the ways that governments can make cities more attractive is to stop over-regulating urban entrepreneurs. An appalling thing about America is that we regulate the entrepreneurship of the poor so much more tightly than we regulate the entreprenuership of the rich. If you want to start your internet phenomenon in your Harvard College dorm, you can have a billion users before any regulator knows you exist. Starting a small convenience store that sells milk products requires dozens of permits. People without fancy computer science degrees tend to be entrepreneurs in the real world, not cyberspace, and this leads to a very different level of regulatory oversight.

Governments must provide safety. In the 1960s and 1970s, New York decided they wanted to run a local welfare system. New York's leaders wanted their cops to stop being mean to people, which is entirely understandable. But there is danger in a leftward local shift at a moment when exit—to suburbia and the sunbelt—had become easier. Companies do not like paying high local taxes. Upper middle-class urbanites do not like crime. By the thousands they voted with their feet and left cities.

I fear a repeat of this phenomenon today. There is an understandable desire to right historic wrongs, but remote work and the ability to relocate makes cities especially vulnerable. Cities must prioritize public safety and quality of life.

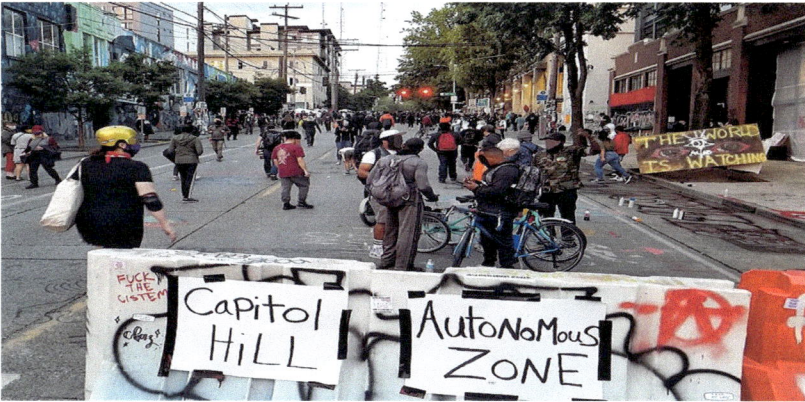

Public Safety is Not Optional — which means investing in the police, not defunding them.

Photo by Ochlo

In the aftermath of the terrible murder of George Floyd, a bevy of unwise public policies came to the fore. The defund the police movement made little sense then or now. The idea that it was acceptable to have autonomous zones where the police did not interfere is similarly bizarre.

The right lesson to take from George Floyd's tragic murder is that we must expect our police to fulfill two mandates. The first mandate is that police must ensure our safety when we walk the streets at night. Typically, the rich are at less risk from crime, and so failing to stop crime particularly harms the most vulnerable urbanites.

The second mandate is that police must treat all our citizens with respect. We are all worthy of dignity. We want to make sure that our police are respecting people. This dual mandate for police—safety and dignity—is doable. I am proud of the way the Boston Police Department has evolved over the decades to manage to deliver both things. They were very different in the 1980s. But this evolution occurred not by spending less, but by spending more.

There is no free lunch in government service. If you want a dual mandate, you are going to need to spend more rather than less. You are also going to need to manage the force better and measure not just crime levels, but how the police treat citizens. Cities should also consider engaging in audit studies in which you check how the police are treating people. Body cameras are a great tool for monitoring officer behavior.

Managing our Infrastructure (joint with Lindsey Currier and Gabriel Kreindler)

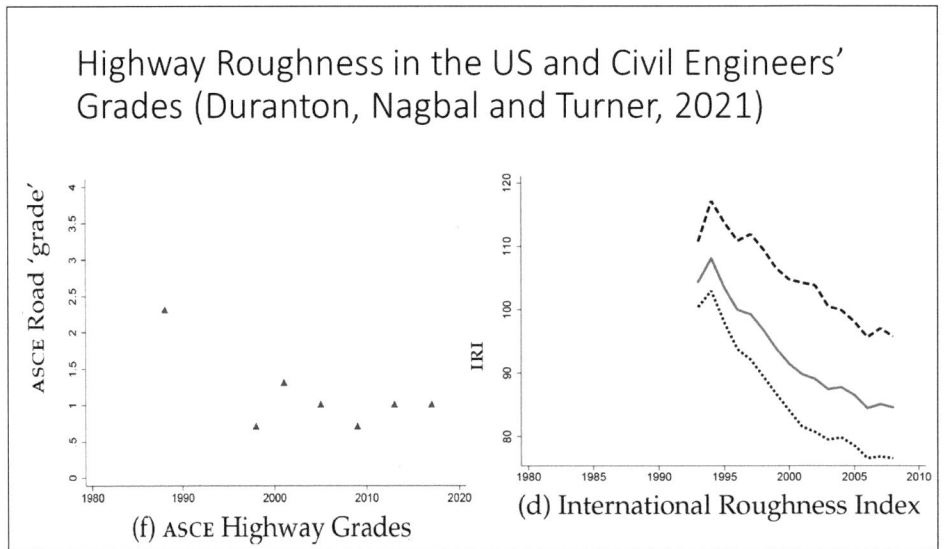

Highway Roughness in the US and Civil Engineers' Grades (Duranton, Nagbal and Turner, 2021)

(f) ASCE Highway Grades

(d) International Roughness Index

Road quality and infrastructure are significant governmental tasks. Infrastructure may be less exciting than other topics we have discussed, but our infrastructure's quality matters. For the last forty years, the American Society of Civil Engineers has told us that our highways had been getting worse. In the 1980s, they gave us a B-. Now they have downgraded our score to a D. The Department of Transportation, however, has been sending out trucks at night with accelerometers to measure road quality. They have shown that our highways have gotten a lot smoother. Over the same period that the ASCE has been arguing that we need to spend trillions and trillions of dollars more on infrastructure, our highways have gotten smoother.

In my daily commute, my highway drives are smooth, but when I get off the highway, particularly after months of winter, the roads are rough. Yet we have not had widespread measures of bumpiness until now.

We have gotten access to the universe of Uber drivers' accelerometers' data for August 2021. Our cell phones have accelerometers that re-right your cell phone when you start tilting it in different directions. All the Uber drivers beam that information back to Uber headquarters where their engineers have figured out how to filter from the data a measure of much the phone is bumping up or down.

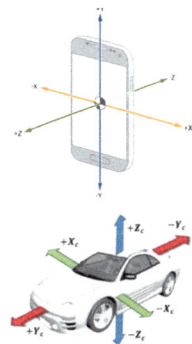

Data: Raw Uber Smartphone Vertical Acc Data

- Accelerometer data from smartphones of active Uber drivers during Uber trips (~ 5Hz)
  - Uber proprietary algorithm to re-align axes: vertical acceleration – measures **bumpiness of the trip**

- Map-matched to road segments covering roughly a block
  - Based on Open Street Map (OSM) road segments

- Data periods:
  - entire US (August 2021)
  - Chicago (April 2018 and March-August 2021)

From the data we can get a usable measure. This is a time series of a single drive from downtown Chicago to O'Hare: bumpy at the beginning, smooth on the highway, bumpy at the end. We can then go from there to measures of local road roughness across America. From this, we can tell you which metropolitan areas are rougher.

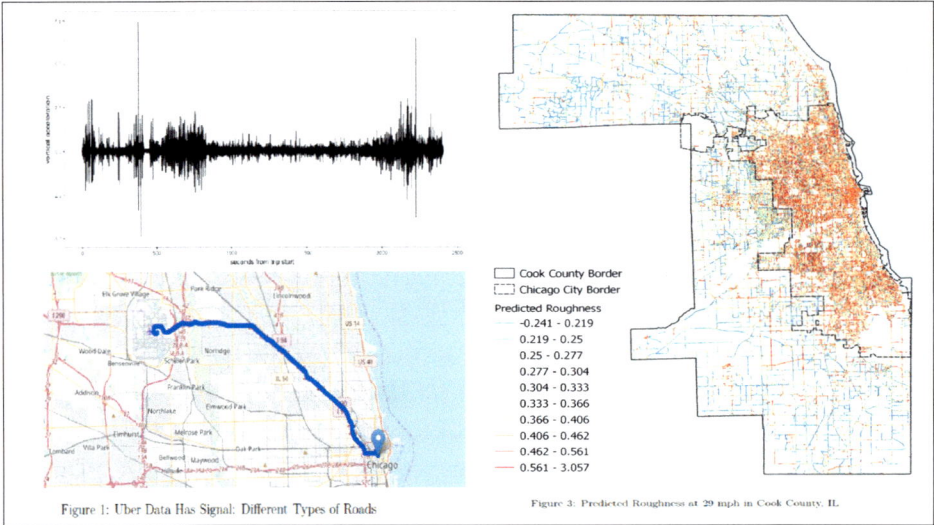

Figure 1: Uber Data Has Signal: Different Types of Roads

Figure 3: Predicted Roughness at 29 mph in Cook County, IL

The coasts are generally rougher than the interior. Houston and New Orleans are terrible, possibly because of the clay in the soil, which absorbs water, expands, and ruins the road. We can then estimate how much American drivers dislike bumpiness. We all can

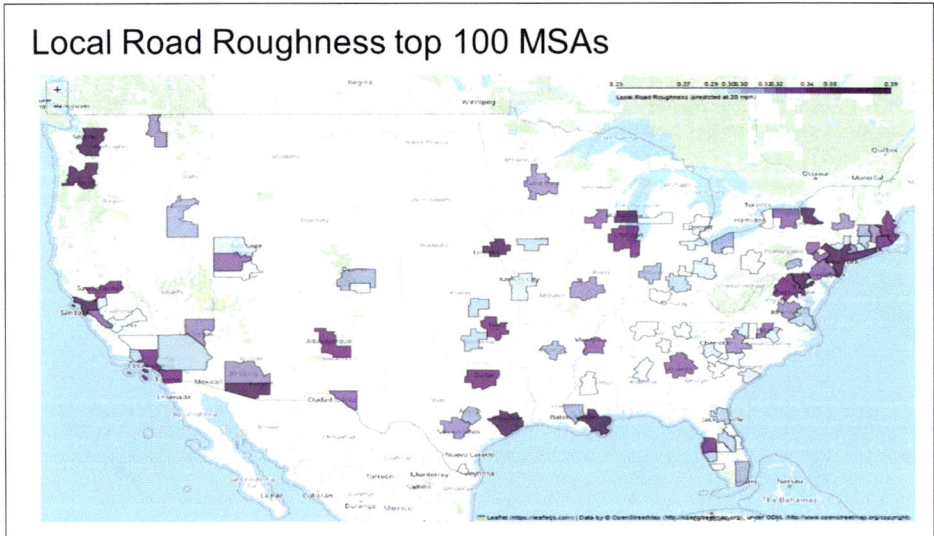

Local Road Roughness top 100 MSAs

smooth our drives by slowing down, but that is costly because we waste time. The extent to which drivers slow down in response to salient changes in roughness generates a measure of the willingness to pay to avoid roughness. We looked at town borders to calculate the relationship between speeds and roughness.

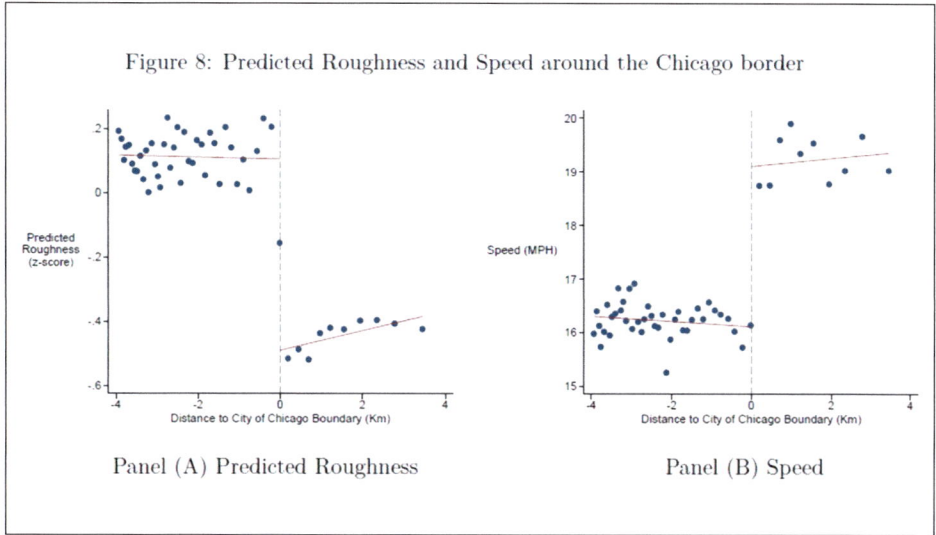

Figure 8: Predicted Roughness and Speed around the Chicago border

Panel (A) Predicted Roughness

Panel (B) Speed

This figure represents the border between Chicago and its wealthy neighbors like Evanston. The richer suburbs' roads are much smoother than Chicago's. This should be clear from the shift in "predicted roughness" on the left. On the right, we show the shift in speeds when the roads get smoother. From that shift, we can estimate a willingness-to-pay-for-smooth-roads. We are not measuring a total social willingness to pay, but the drivers' dislike of bumpiness. There may be positive or negative externalities to others from driving more quickly.

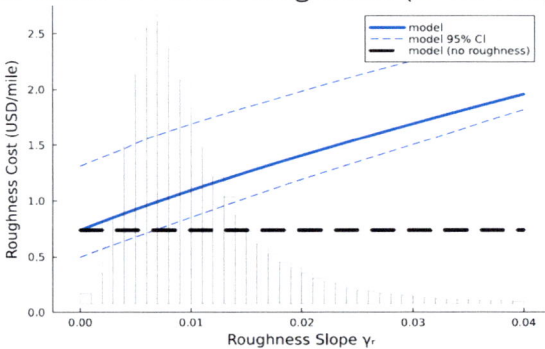

Total User Costs of Road Roughness (1 mile segment)

- Median roughness has cost of 0.31 USD / mile
- Cost 1 SD higher road roughness is 0.23 USD / mile CI: [0.2, 0.3]
- Using the road resurfacing data, costs are roughly double

Inequality: Road Roughness, Income, and Race

- Consider a HH that drives 3,000 miles per year on local roads

- Going from 100% White to 100% Black associated with 318 dollars per year additional cost due to roughness

	Dependent variable:					
	Cost (USD per mile)					
	(1)	(2)	(3)	(4)	(5)	(6)
ln median income	−0.043***	−0.052***	−0.017***			
	(0.001)	(0.001)	(0.002)			
fraction Black				0.106***	0.104***	0.016***
				(0.003)	(0.003)	(0.004)
fraction Hispanic				0.090***	0.077***	0.031***
				(0.003)	(0.004)	(0.004)
fraction Asian				0.085***	0.038***	−0.034***
				(0.007)	(0.007)	(0.008)
Climate controls	Yes			Yes		
MSA Fixed effects		Yes			Yes	
Town Fixed effects			Yes			Yes
Observations	32,967	33,134	33,134	32,967	33,134	33,134
Adjusted R^2	0.053	0.144	0.346	0.073	0.144	0.346

These are our estimates. The baseline cost of driving is about seventy cents per mile, which represents the drivers' time plus the gas cost. Bumpiness typically adds about fifty percent to the cost. We can then correlate the bumpiness costs with neighborhood income and demographics. We estimate that if a household drives about three thousand miles per year on local roads, then moving from a one hundred percent white neighborhood to a one hundred percent African-American neighborhood is associated with drivers experiencing $318 worth of extra pain in road roughness. These differences are almost all across town rather than within town. Poorer people live in towns and towns tend to have rougher roads.

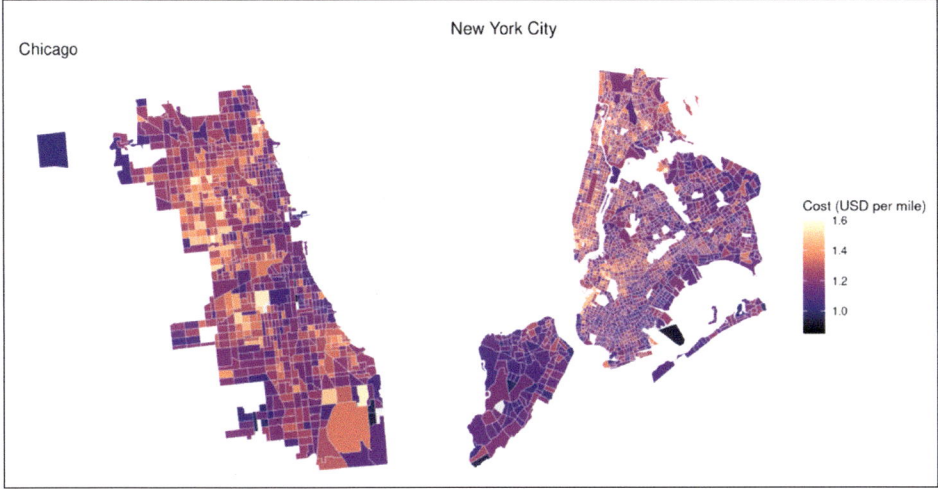

In big cities, typically rich people have roads that are just as rough as poor people. This figure shows New York City. The lighter areas are really bumpy. In Tribeca, the area close to Wall Street, there are very rough roads, and they also have really rich people. Often rich people live near and in the urban core to save commute times, but those are also the areas with the highest number of trucks and the bumpiest roads. In Chicago, you have a slightly different pattern, because there is a truck-intensive industrial area in the west that is also really bumpy. There is more of a gradient with poverty there.

It is possible to fit this into a cost benefit analysis and figure out how much we should be repaving, but it turns out there is a much simpler way to improve America's roads.

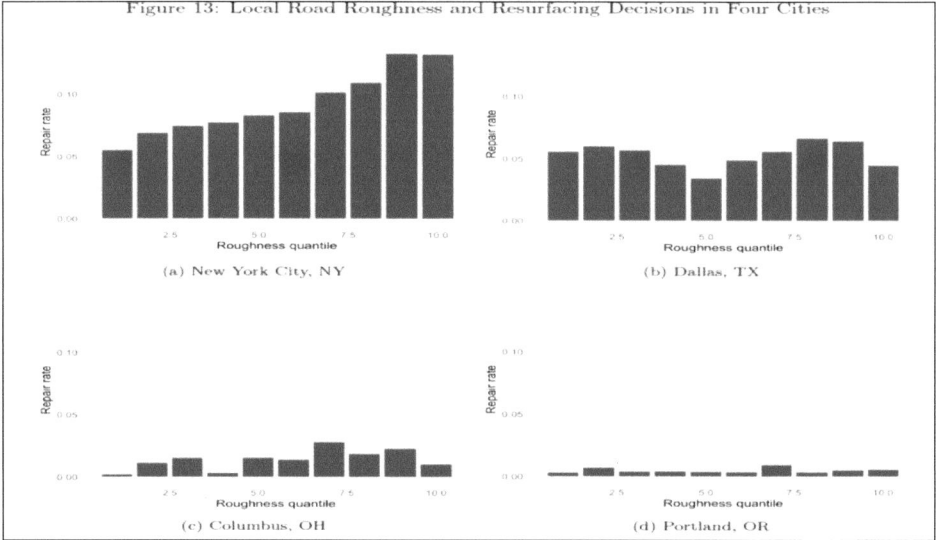

(a) New York City, NY

(b) Dallas, TX

(c) Columbus, OH

(d) Portland, OR

This figure shows the probability of being repaved over the eight months after we measured roughness as a function of roughness at a pre-period. In three of the four, there is virtually no correlation between probability of being repaved and the initial roughness. We seem to be doing nothing to target rougher roads in these cities. The simple formula for making America's local roads smoother is to be smarter about where you repave. Even in New York, where there is a slight correlation, it is weak.

Survey with 120 towns and cities in US

	Massachusetts	Rest of US
Panel A: Percent of Roads that Receive the Resurfacing they Require		
> 90%	0.11	0.05
70-90%	0.05	0.11
50-70%	0.05	0.13
30-50%	0.42	0.06
< 30%	0.32	0.62
Unsure	0.05	0.03
Panel B: Spending on Resurfacing vs Preventative Maintenance		
> 90% on resurfacing	0.11	0.20
70 - 90% on resurfacing	0.68	0.47
50 - 70% on resurfacing	0.16	0.18
50% on resurfacing	0.00	0.02
30 - 50% on resurfacing	0.00	0.04
< 30% on resurfacing	0.00	0.09
Unsure	0.05	0.01
Observations	19	101

We surveyed 120 cities and towns. Typically, towns decide when to repave their roads by having some measure for documenting roughness, which may be a visual measure that is only weakly correlated with speeds. Then they have a mandate which says all the roads that fail on this test are supposed to be repaved. Now what percent of roads are repaved in these cities? Sixty-two percent of our U.S. sample of cities say that less than thirty percent of the roads that need repaving are being repaved. Our discussions with public works groups suggests that there is little targeting of that thirty percent. The mandate is unrealistic. Our big less for improving American infrastructure is just to repave the bumpy roads first.

Conclusion

Dynamism in America requires two changes. First, governments need to decrease unwise regulation, including regulation of large or small businesses and building. Second, our governments need to do their work more effectively.

For these changes to occur, our citizens must ask their governments to do more. A simple example of government underperformance is poor targeting of road repaving. But we also need to figure out why our roads are so expensive. We care a lot about eliminating corruption in road contracts, but we care not at all about reducing prices. We end up adding a lot of sludge that makes it impossible to get more competitive bidding and firms' easier entry into this process.

Policing also needs to improve. We need to make sure that our streets are safe, and that simultaneously, our police treat everyone with respect. We should incarcerate fewer people for minor crimes.

Public schooling is also a major problem. We need to ensure America continues to have the level of opportunity that we want it to have. Education has been our traditional engine for that. I am open to other engines, but skills are the bedrock on which individual town, city, or national success rests. We are not going to be a strong nation unless our skill levels lead the world.

But here in Texas it is impossible not to feel confident and optimistic. Despite the challenges we face, we should not count this country out yet. Tremendous dynamism is possible. But we need to take on the hard work of tearing down the regulations that make us weak and improving the quality of public services that will support our natural strengths.

4. Sludge, Stagnation, and Dynamism

Cass Sunstein

Sludge consists of the obstacles one encounters when trying to begin a new company, trying to innovate, or trying to start an entrepreneurial activity that might change the lives of thousands or tens of thousands.[1] If the government requires entrepreneurs to find a license before they can start their landscape architect business, for example, they are encountering sludge. That sludge might take six weeks, six months, or a year to resolve. It might involve forms that are unintelligible, it might impair economic growth, and it might be an obstacle to one's sense of individual dignity. There are permit requirements all over the world that reduce freedom and crush welfare. They are dynamism's enemy because they make it difficult for people to do things that will improve their lives.

A number	11 billion hours
	Whoa
	A question: In other countries?

Here is the result of the United States government's recent sludge audit. The question is how many hours in paperwork burdens does the United States impose on people? The answer is now in the vicinity of 10-11 billion hours. These billions of hours have a considerable human cost. The government imposes them on students, higher-ed administrators, doctors, nurses, hospital workers, patients, and truck drivers. People all over the United States who are trying to go about their day and forms too confusing and daunting to navigate occupy that day are facing sludge. Parenthetically, by way of footnote, the editors of an academic journal asked me to contribute an article. The invitation is an honor, but the website is so sludge pervaded, I am considering refusing to submit because sludge has made it too difficult.

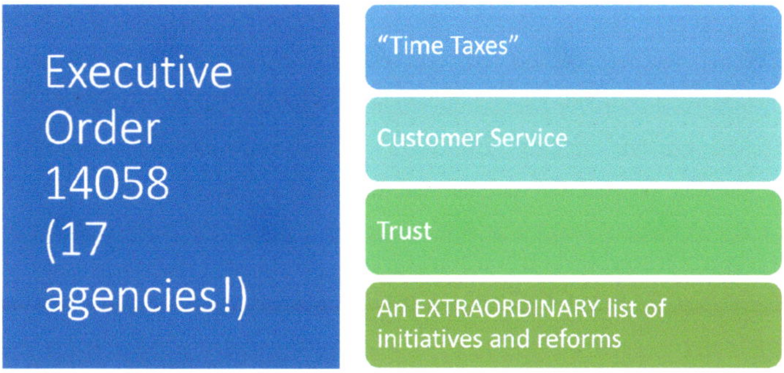

Executive Order 14058 (17 agencies!)

- "Time Taxes"
- Customer Service
- Trust
- An EXTRAORDINARY list of initiatives and reforms

That said, there is some good news: Joe Biden's Executive Order 14058. You've probably never heard of it because even though Republicans like it, they have no incentive to cheer the current president. The Democrats' focus is on other things, so they do not have any incentive to cheer either. It calls out the time taxes sludge imposes on people and suggests that the imposition is predominantly made on people who are trying to do business, to innovate, or to get services from the U.S. government. E.O. 14058 includes an extraordinary list of initiatives and reforms. It is based on the idea that the best way to obtain trust is to earn it. If you do something that makes customer service better, whether you are a startup or the Department of Transportation, then trust, as a performance byproduct, will increase.

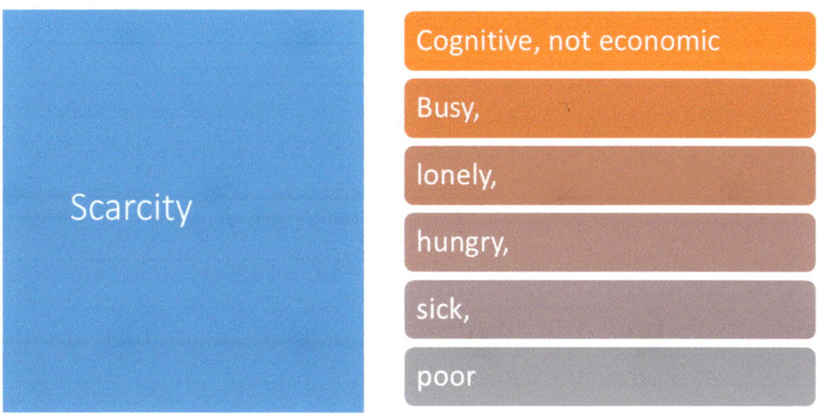

Scarcity

- Cognitive, not economic
- Busy,
- lonely,
- hungry,
- sick,
- poor

We will now turn to behavioral science. Cognitive scarcity is a feature the human brain shares with cats, dogs, horses, and mosquitoes. Cognitive scarcity compliments economic scarcity. The number of things to which our focus and energy can attend is a subset of the number of things that are relevant. That means we must set priorities and if you are busy, because you are an entrepreneur trying to get started, or an innovator who is focusing on your innovations, or if you are lonely because you do not have friends, or if you're hungry because you do not have food, or if you are really not feeling very well, these priorities are often set extremely rapidly. If you are poor, the problem of cognitive scarcity jumps sky high. If you are hungry, when I flash the letters CDAEQRKLMA on the screen, you will immediately see the word "cake," because because the letters C A K E shot out from that random assortment. This is based on data, not speculation. Had you just eaten lunch, you would not see "cake" among those letters. If you were hungry and focused on food, you would see CAKE, and the number of other priorities you would be able to focus on would be small. Take this as a poignant but not comprehensive reason sludge can be a growth barrier.

What you see, if you are hungry

What seems to happen to your intelligence, if you have an economic challenge

What seems to happen to your executive function

Equity

If you are poor, and asked to solve an economic problem that you personally face before you take an intelligence test, your intelligence falls by eight or nine I.Q. points, which is the same point drop people who did not sleep the night before the test experience. If you are not poor and you are asked to solve a challenging economic problem before you take an intelligence test, your intelligence does not fall at all. If you are poor and asked to solve an economic challenge that you personally face and then take a test that measures your self control capacity—your executive function— it collapses, because executive function requires cognitive plenitude, not cognitive scarcity. When asked to solve an economic problem, people facing economic distress experience fluid intelligence and self control diminution. This is a problem people in economic distress face, but this diminution also has parallels in people who have other kinds of challenges, including people who have cognitive scarcity just because they are very busy.

Scarcity and sludge combined is horrible. Busy people who are suffering from time scarcity or poor people who are suffering from resource scarcity face the most sludge. This is a cruelty that those who impose sludge do not typically intend. It is also a cruelty with severe growth consequences in both wealthy and poor countries. By stymying efforts to make changes or introduce efficiencies and reforms that would make more and better employment, sludge has obstructed U.S. growth and job creation. Starting today, we need a sludge reduction movement born of social science research, work in business schools, and work by concerned people who want to ensure opportunity for all.

My coauthor and friend Daniel Kahneman recently died. I want to make a little note on his final paper. It is a triumph of the human spirit that he wrote at approximately ninety years old. It grew out of a provocative paper he wrote with Angus Deaton, which said that well being increases in step with income up to about $70,000 or $90,000 per year, at which point it levels off. The paper suggested that if you are poor, your measured well being in terms of how you experience life jumps rapidly, but after $70,000 or $90,000, it flattens. (Bracket for now the measurement reliability for well being and just notice that this was Deaton and Kahneman's finding.)

A few years ago, a graduate student named Matthew Killingsworth wrote a paper based on data more refined than that Deaton and Kahneman used. He showed that their conclusions were wrong: in terms of well being, more money really is better. Kahneman's reaction to this fundamental attack on his paper was to call Killingsworth and offer to co-write a specified hypothesis paper to see whose findings were correct. Their collaboration would be adversarial; they would agree on how the data would have to look for one or the other's findings to be convincing and they would agree to interrogate the data with their competing hypotheses in mind. Killingsworth, probably astounded to get this call from the great Kahneman, agreed. The completed paper, which emerged just a few months ago, showed that Killingsworth was more correct than Kahneman.

The basic finding is that measured well being keeps increasing alongside economic increase. That is a point for Killingsworth with one qualification: the people at the bottom fifteen percent of the happiness distribution who are struggling with well being saw their life get better and better between $10,000 and $100,000 per year before flattening. Why does their measured well being flatten after $100,000? Kahneman and Killingsworth were not sure, so they only speculated cautiously that those suffering from depression or anxiety really need to earn more than $20,000 per year and more income is better, but then after $100,000, those mental health struggles remain. Take this paper to be a tribute. It is state of the art on the relationship between dynamism related to economic growth and measures of well being that are not monetary.

Less Sludge:

Enroll in Trusted Traveler Programs to Expedite Your International Travel

Welcome to the official U.S. Customs and Border Protection (CBP) website, where international travelers can apply for Trusted Traveler Programs. These programs allow for expedited processing into the United States. To be a Trusted Traveler you must be pre-approved and determined to be low risk.

Get Started

I've already started applying

I'm already a program member

Many of you arrived here by airplane. Those who did I hope used the traveler reduction strategy TSA PreCheck. On average, it reduces the time to get through security to only five to seven minutes. TSA PreCheck's monetized welfare benefit for travelers is high. I also hope many of you use Global Entry, which is a sludge reduction strategy compatible with U.S. government national security goals for people hurrying home to the U.S. What America now needs, if promoting innovation is a goal, is the functional equivalent of Global Entry for everything. That would be a world with much less sludge.

We test an intervention to increase enrollment of low-income students at the University of Michigan.

The intervention was designed to address problems that affect the college choices of low-income, high-achieving students

We contact students (as well as their parents and principals) with an encouragement to apply and a promise of four years of free tuition and fees upon admission

· Treated students were more than twice as likely to apply to (67 percent vs. 26 percent) and enroll at (27 percent vs. 12 percent) the University of Michigan.
· Effects persist through two years of follow-up.
· The intervention closed by half the income gaps in college choice among Michigan's high-achieving students.
· Wow.

Dynamism is also connected to the educational domain. Here is a staggering paper from 2018 that shows a problem at the University of Michigan—one of our greatest public universities give or take Texas or Berkeley. Michigan had a problem. The students who were attending were smart and high income. It was not the world's worst problem, but smart, low-income students were not attending, which is baffling, because if they applied, they received free tuition and fees on admission. The problem was that they were not applying, so Michigan intervened to take away the sludge. The intervenors told the students, parents, and principals that if low-income students applied, they would receive free admission, free tuition, a nice song, and no fees. All the intervention said was that students did not have to do anything to get into Michigan.

The result was that application likelihood and enrollment more than doubled. The effect persisted through two years. It is staggering that this intervention closed by half the income gap in college choice among Michigan's high achieving students. No money was necessary. All that Michigan needed to close the gap was information about something where information acquisition would have entailed the incursion of sludge. As an aside, there is also a simple intervention to reduce U.S. gun deaths—a three to five day waiting period.

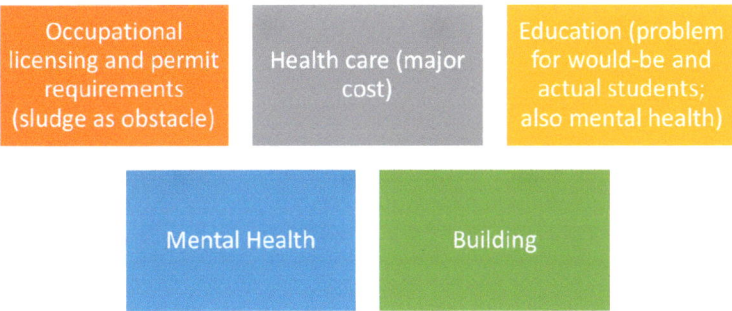

Occupational licensing and permit requirements (sludge as obstacle)	Health care (major cost)	Education (problem for would-be and actual students; also mental health)
Mental Health	Building	

Occupational licensing and permit requirements are sludge. Sludge is public enemy number one when it comes to building things, such as residential housing. And we need to build a lot of things in the United States. Sludge also fills our healthcare and educational systems. David Cutler has found that sludge is a significant contributor to U.S. healthcare costs. I had lunch with six students at a very distinguished university about eighteen months ago and asked them about their university's healthcare system. Four of them said it was great. One student said that it had not been great for her because she suffers from depression and treatment required navigating so many processes and talking to so many people and filling out so many forms that the process itself started to make her really, really depressed. She ended up giving up on trying to find treatment at her university.

Millions of low-income people fail to claim tax benefits for which they are eligible, in part because the rules governing the benefits are extraordinarily complex.

Special Supplemental Nutrition Program for Women, Infants, and Children:

In a recent year, more than 2.4 million infants in the United States were eligible for WIC. 80 percent of eligible infants did not participate in the program. 50 percent of eligible pregnant women were not covered.

Now we will turn to the problem of desperation. Opinions on the Supplemental Nutrition Program for Women, Infants and Children may differ, but I personally love the program. In a recent year, more than 2.4 million infants in the U.S. were eligible. Eighty percent didn't participate in the program and sludge prevented fifty percent of eligible pregnant women from participating. Getting into the program requires navigating processes. Keep in mind the problem of scarcity, which the relevant population in particular faces.

Agency	Burden Hours
Department of the Treasury/Internal Revenue Service (IRS)	7357.22
Department of Health and Human Services (HHS)	695.88
Securities and Exchange Commission (SEC)	224.89
Department of Transportation (DOT)	214.21
Department of Homeland Security (DHS)	203.39
Environmental Protection Agency (EPA)	156.89
Department of Labor (DOL)	144.71
Federal Trade Commission (FTC)	135.37
Department of Agriculture (USDA)	127.55
Department of Education	90.84

Courtesy of 1980, we have a law called the Paperwork Reduction Act, but it has not fulfilled its promise. It was my job to oversee the Paperwork Reduction Act for four years. My presentation today is somewhat of a mea culpa. Keep in mind that the 11 billion hours of paperwork the government imposes has remained fairly steady over time. The national sludge audit uncovered at the macro level what this slide is showing you right now. The Department of Education imposes 90 million annual hours of paperwork burdens on people, including students, administrators, and professors. The Department of Agriculture imposes 127 million hours on farmers, many of whom have little time to fill out forms. The Department of Labor imposes 144 million hours on workers, employers, and others who fall in a general category. The Department of Transportation has north of 200 million hours. The Department of Treasury is the prize winner at 7 billion hours. These are numbers, but keep in mind the high level of human distress these obstacles and barriers cause.

Because we have been with each other for part of a day now, I will tell you a slightly personal story. I am speaking to you here in my academic capacity, but I am also a Department of Homeland Security bureaucrat. A personage—not just a random person—in Washington, D.C., called me a few months ago asking me to help his son get a green card so that he could visit his dying grandmother. I said I could not help. The personage who called me is well known, important, and amazing. My ethics caused me to feel very guilty about my no answer. The personage was enraged that I could not help. The rage affected me, so I called my colleagues at D.H.S. and asked if there was anything they could do to help. They told me there was nothing they could do. I backed off and told my friend I couldn't help. In response to that unwelcome news, my friend lamented that after spending hours on D.H.S.'s website trying to speak to someone directly, it was too difficult to navigate. I gave the only answer I could think of: call a lawyer. The personage did call a lawyer and called me back the next day and told me that the lawyer knew exactly what to do and solved the problem in ten minutes. But this was not a triumphant call; it was an outrage call. What about everyone who does not know to call a lawyer? That is a great question.

This number-pervaded chart shows countless everyday stories exactly like that. Some involve little companies trying to get workers from a country where they're available. Others involve someone trying to start a business who needs a permit and has no idea how to get it. Texas needs a paperwork reduction act, Mississippi needs one, and California really needs one. My state Massachusetts needs one. The paperwork reduction act should have all and more of the Federal Paperwork Reduction Act's content.

	Low Friction	High Friction
Good	Helpful "Make It Easy" Nudge (eg, simplification; airport maps; automatic enrollment in good pension plan) (1)	Deliberating-Promoting Nudge (eg, "are you sure you want to?"; cooling off period) (2)
Bad	Harmful "Make It Easy" Nudge (eg, automatic enrollment in costly terrible not-good program) (3)	**Sludge (eg, form-filling nightmares; permitting nightmares; long waiting times for drivers' licenses or visas) (4)**

What is the relationship between sludge and nudge? How are they connected with one another? I will define sludge as friction stemming from paperwork and associated burdens, time spent standing in line, in-person interview requirements, complicated forms, and places the government requires you to go. These are all sludge. This chart might clarify. A low-friction, make-it-easy nudge includes radically simplified processes and automatic enrollment in something that benefits people. There is also harmful make-it-easy nudge. An automatic enrollment program exists, for example, that entitles you to ten percent off if you ever go to a war-zone and want to stay in a local hotel. It is fraud. People do not want to go to those hotels, but they are convinced to enroll in those programs. And enrollment is really easy. Consider that a nudge for evil.

Then there are deliberation promoting nudges, such as an are-you-sure-you-want-to, or a cooling off period. Those cooling off periods are sludge. They impose friction for good, but my focus is on the chart's bottom right—permitting nightmares, long waiting times, filling out forms, Stephen King novels. I follow Stephen King on X, but he does not follow me. I really want him to write a book about sludge and make it really scary. I am hopeful that many of you are thinking right now that the sludge Texas, or Austin, or Washington D.C. imposes might have a purpose beyond simply creating terrible burdens for people. Let us now discuss five defenses of how sludge attempts to balance dynamism and other salutary goals optimally.

Most interesting: Promoting reflection/deliberation ("are you sure you want to"; cooling off periods; waiting to choose and promoting deliberation, see Imas et al.; the complex case of abortion)	Most important: Program integrity (and how to think about that; complex tradeoff))	Most pragmatic: Acquiring useful data
Most boring: Privacy/consent	Most provocative: Ordeals as a sorting mechanism? (Nope. Nah.)	

Sludge's most provocative defense is that ordeals can be a sorting mechanism. Suppose that Taylor Swift is playing at UT Austin the night after next. How are we going to sort access? We could impose an ordeal on people, meaning that if you start standing in line at approximately 3:30 today, and you are toward the front of the line, you have concert access. If that is a sensible sorting mechanism, it is because time—like money—can measure intensity of need or desire. It ends up reasonably sorting who deserves access to the thing. Data is synced as far as suggesting that this rationale is potentially true in principle but does not work in practice. It is typically very ineffective as a sorting mechanism.

The most boring justification for sludge is privacy and consent: you require people to provide information because we do not want the government accessing that information without people's knowledge or approval. That is completely fair, but it does not justify existing sludge levels. The most pragmatic justification is that if the government is giving money to people to do something, start a technological enterprise, for example, the government needs to acquire performance data. How is the enterprise going? The most important justification is program integrity. We want to ensure that deserving people are receiving permits. It is possible we should excise permit requirements entirely, but so long as they are in place, we want to make sure the sorting is the right sorting. Promoting deliberation is another sludge justification. That sludge is are-you-sure-you-want-to sludge. It is designed to ensure that people aren't reckless or impulsive.

Environmental protection and worker safety are also familiar sludge justifications. I am going to tell you a personal story about nineteen-year-old me and the National Environmental Policy Act. When I was a college student, I worked for the Army Corps of Engineers writing environmental impact statements, which had the honorable goal of promoting consideration of significant environmental effects before the government issued permits. I saw very intimately that the government designed these statements, which impose sludge on the private and public sector, to stop development in ways that were often not environmentally magnificent, but instead promoted the interests of self-interested private groups. This does not suggest that we should end the National Environmental Policy Act, but we should rethink it with the goal of ensuring sludge is at optimal levels.

Let us talk about how to do that. For Texas, Oklahoma, Georgia, New Jersey, New York especially, we need to manage the existing sludge stock with determination and laughter. There is also a flow of new sludge that we must ferociously restrain. How do we manage this new sludge flow? First, we need a quantitative cost benefit test, or a qualitative test if a quantitative one is not possible. If the government imposes sludge at X amount on people who are trying to do X, what would we lose if we cut that in half? These are fully answerable questions. I have talked about Global Entry and TSA PreCheck. Both of those programs emerged from cost benefit tests, which suggested that in both cases, they are close to no regrets policies. Since we need someone to manage those programs, they are not entirely all benefit and no costs, but they come close. Cost benefit balancing with respect to the flow of new sludge is good for America.

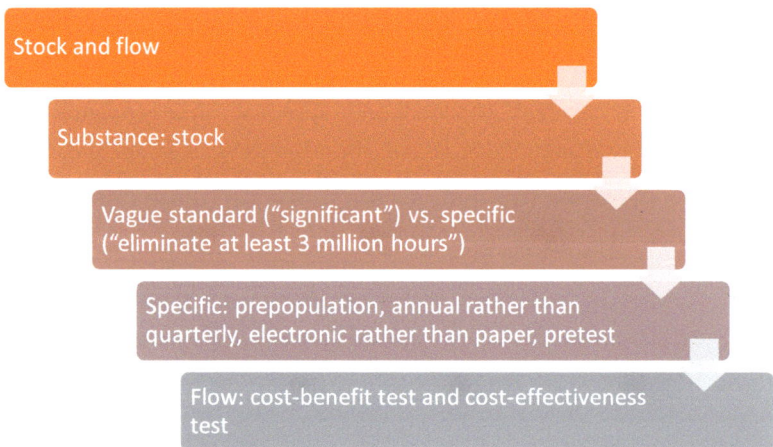

Stock and flow

Substance: stock

Vague standard ("significant") vs. specific ("eliminate at least 3 million hours")

Specific: prepopulation, annual rather than quarterly, electronic rather than paper, pretest

Flow: cost-benefit test and cost-effectiveness test

We can also do a lot to manage the existing sludge flow stock. One possibility is to impose a vague standard that requires significant reductions from every part of state government by a certain date. Specific standards are also an option. They could require, for example, eliminating at least 3 million hours in paperwork burdens by a specific date. We could require specificity not just in terms of hours, but in terms of concrete reforms, such as requiring that forms are pre-populated, so people do not have to fill them out, or that forms will be annual rather than quarterly and filed electronically rather than through paper. We could also do pre-tests on existing forms to see if the actual, real-world time burden exceeds the anticipated time burden. If we find that it does, we could eliminate a certain number of forms.

USCIS and barriers and burdens — over 7000 comments

On May 3, 2022, U.S. Citizenship and Immigration Services (USCIS) announced a Temporary Final Rule (TFR) that would increase the automatic extension period for Employment Authorization Documents (EADs) from 180 days to 540 days.

Here is something that Citizenship and Natural Immigration Services (USCIS) did: it issued a Federal Register notice asking what barriers and burdens people faced when dealing with the office. They emphatically included businesses and entrepreneurs in this inquiry. They received 7000 comments. USCIS marched through all 7000 comments trying to find the ones to which they could manageably respond. The result was USCIS's rule, issued in 2022, that increased the automatic extension period for employment authorization from 180 days to 540 days. American employers danced in the streets because their workers could continue working rather than going to file. The workers themselves were not dancing, but they did breathe a big sigh of relief.

Here is a suggestion for permitting requirements of various sorts; we should consider doubling or tripling the length of time that people can enjoy their existing permit. If the permit is issued for four years, we should extend it to eight. That automatically removes backlogs and leads to relevant dynamism increases. The Department of Homeland Security issued a 20-million-hour challenge, saying we must eliminate 20 million hours in the paperwork burdens we impose on people in short order. If you remember the earlier slide listed D.H.S.'s paperwork burden total as 200 million, so this reform required an aggressive goal of a nearly instant ten% decrease. D.H.S. beat that; they eliminated 21 million hours of sludge. Some people I know in D.C. who deal with the government have noticed this change because they are getting approvals within a week rather than a year. That is sludge reduction.

Executive orders are usually just a few pages of high-level writing. Executive Order 14058 is very unusual because it's lengthy and says such things as "eliminate permit requirements," "make things automatic," "simplify for farmers," and "if people are eligible for this, and you know that because they've applied and they're also eligible for that, then don't make them apply, they're in automatically." Here is an example: E.O. 14058 requires the Secretary of State to design a new online passport renewal experience that eliminates the need to mail anything. This is not going to drive a lot of U.S. innovation, but it will remove much of the frustration and burden imposed on people whom the current systems require to show up in an unfamiliar place and deal with unfamiliar people when they are just hoping to get to London for vacation.

- The Administrator of the United States Agency for International Development (USAID) shall review and revise, as appropriate, regulations, forms, instructions, or other sources of guidance relating to the application for grants and cooperative agreements in countries in which USAID works to ensure that
- such policies are clear and intelligible, do not contain unjustified administrative burdens or excessive paperwork requirements, and do not place undue burdens on local organizations and underserved communities.

This is Administrator Power, who happens to be my wife. The E.O. 14058 directs her to revise and review regulations, forms, instructions, etc., so that countries in USAID Works can receive the resources to which they have a legal right. It might be people in Ukraine who are dealing with war, it might be people in Pakistan who are dealing with flooding, it might be people in a nation trying to stand on its own feet with development. The idea is to eliminate the sludge. Let me tell you a very inside baseball story. As the Biden Administration was writing the order, there were a lot of interagency processes making sure it was okay. I had some engagement with the USAID process and having such engagement, I would ask my wife if everything in the process was correct. Both as a good bureaucrat and as a good spouse, you do not inflict on an agency head to whom you are married an executive order that she hates. That would not be good for the marriage or for the country. She told me that the order was coming along well, she was happy with it, and it was consistent with her agency's goal. Then during the interagency process, there was a question about whether USAID was happy with the order. And I was pleased to be able to say that the agency was happy and enthusiastic about the order. And in response, Administrator Power issued a 3 million hour challenge to her staff to eliminate 3 million hours of paperwork burdens with the goal of promoting dynamism in the nations with which the United States works.

Finally, a question for all of us: what is the most precious resource human beings have? There are a lot of candidate answers. As the COVID pandemic recedes in our rearview mirror, there is one answer that stands out above all others. It is a four-letter word: time. We should find, in the interests of equality of permission, in the interests of liberty, in the interest of growth, and—tip of the hat to Kahneman—in the interest of welfare, ways to give other human beings more time.

Endnote

[1] Readers are asked to make allowances for what was originally an oral presentation.

Part III
Key Drivers of Dynamic Economies: New Businesses and Housing

5. Recent Patterns of New Business Creation

Ryan Decker

Note: Without implication, this talk relied primarily on research done jointly with John Haltiwanger (University of Maryland and the National Bureau of Economic Research).[1] The analysis and conclusions set forth are those of the author and do not indicate concurrence by other members of the research staff or the Board of Governors of the Federal Reserve System.

Let's start with this chart from a Census Bureau product called the Business Formation Statistics that shows new business applications. The I.R.S. gives data to the Census Bureau on applications for new Employer Identification Numbers (E.I.N.). If you want to start a business, and you plan to become a corporation, or a partnership, or if you are going to be hiring workers, you will need an I.R.S.-issued E.I.N. Even some sole proprietorships

Business applications (thousands)

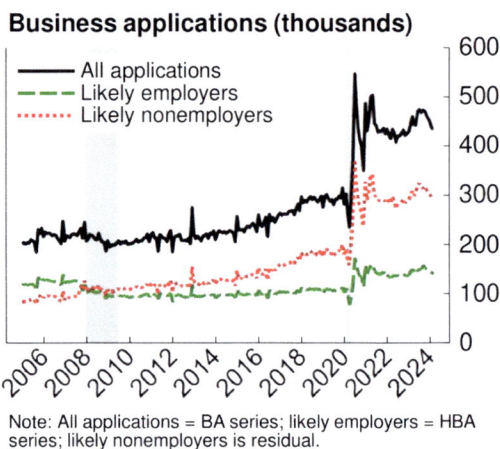

Note: All applications = BA series; likely employers = HBA series; likely nonemployers is residual.

obtain E.I.N.s for various reasons. The I.R.S. compiles these data, ships them over to the Census Bureau, then the Census Bureau takes the dataset, throws out non businesses like trusts and estates, and keeps everything else. Then they report these applications. Now importantly, some of these applications are aspirational. These businesses might not actually do or build anything, but they are all people who have applied for E.I.N.s.

The black line shows total applications. Those are monthly data. The green line shows likely employer applications. The Census Bureau flags some application characteristics, including indicated industry, the legal organizational form, or the intention to hire employees. Likely employer applications is a subset of the total series that have one or more characteristics that tend to be predictive of actual employer business creation. Importantly, this is not a model-based prediction of business entry, but a subset of the applications that tends to move closely with actual firm entry.

There are some very striking and surprising patterns. If you think back to how you felt in March or April 2020, very few of us expected a historic surge in business entry or really anything positive at all, but that is what we got. Initially, there was a dip in these applications, but then they surged to the highest pace on record. The sharp point on the chart is July 2020. Then the first wave eased down throughout the rest of the year. By 2021 however, all these series picked up again, and have remained elevated, even into March 2024.

A striking thing about this is that the likely-employer series moved closely with the likely-non-employers series (the difference between the total and the likely employers). This is surprising because it runs contrary to historic patterns. There are many reasons why "nonemployer entrepreneurship"—i.e., just doing your own thing and not hiring anybody/self-employment—might increase in a weak economic environment. People looking for income in a bad labor environment might try self-employment. Indeed, in the Great Recession, we saw an increase in non-employer entrepreneurship. But the likely employer series is surprising because employer entrepreneurship during recessions tends to plummet. But here we have it moving closely with the likely non-employers.

This surprise led to many questions, some of which we will answer today. First, are these applications serious? Initially many economists were skeptical about what this surge meant. Applying for an E.I.N is easy and low-cost. Maybe people who were working from home or temporarily laid off in summer 2020 with nothing to do were filing for E.I.N.s. It was possible that this surge in applications was meaningless. The concern was that even though these applications series have historically predicted actual employer entry successfully, for the reasons I just said, the pandemic surge could be different.

The next question is even if these are real employer entrants, what happened and why? I do not have rigorous causal analysis on this question today but what I am going to do is use these data to tell pandemic stories. We can make sense of these data in terms of geographic patterns and industry patterns by comparing them to other things we know about the pandemic. I will argue that this surge makes sense, given everything else we know.

I will also touch on productivity. Historically business entry is important for productivity because of how new and innovative ideas spread and accumulate productive resources. But could this time be different? Maybe, for example, these new businesses were lifestyle entrepreneurs who did not have an idea so much as they were looking for a change of pace. And if that is the case, then we might not see the productivity boost from this entry surge that we have seen from past entry surges. And finally, I will talk about longer run trends. My co-author and I and others have done a lot of research in pre-pandemic trends in business entry, I will put us in that context.

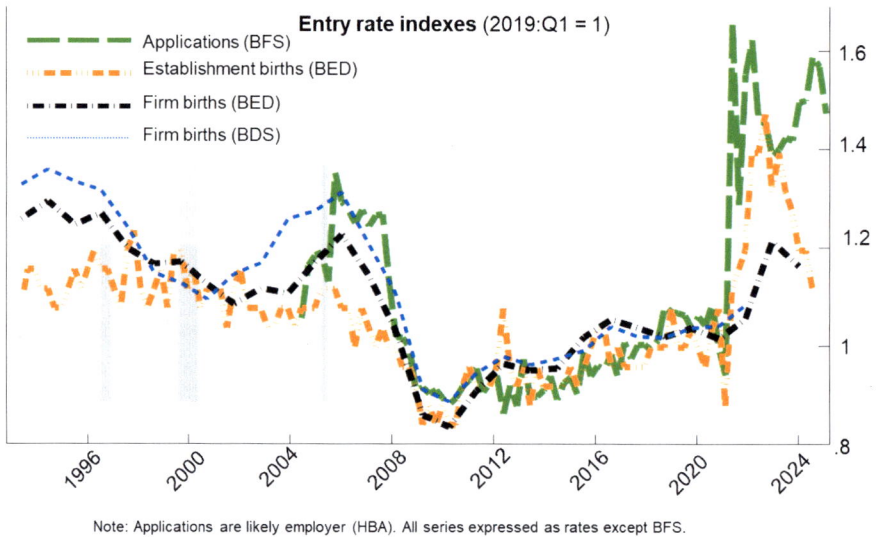

Entry rate indexes (2019:Q1 = 1)

Note: Applications are likely employer (HBA). All series expressed as rates except BFS.

Let's start by answering the first question. Actual employer business creation did, in fact, follow these E.I.N. applications. The chart's green line is the likely employer application series. The orange line is a measure of employer establishment births (quarterly). These are actual business locations with actual formal W-2 employees. Let me clarify a bit of technical jargon first. The word "establishment" has a very precise meaning in U.S. statistical agencies. An "establishment" is any employer business operating location. What does that mean? It means that an "establishment birth" could be the start of a brand-new firm, meaning a new company starting up and hiring people, or alternatively, it could be a new Starbucks location. That distinction is important. We get those data at a quarterly frequency. Starting in the second quarter of 2021, establishment births increased. And they have remained very high, though recently they have started to come down again. But from the second quarter of 2021 through the most recent data in the third quarter of 2023, new establishments were creating a million jobs per quarter. That is an enormous number. And it has played a significant role in labor market stories.

But if these are new Starbucks locations rather than new firms, the implications would be quite different. The black line on the chart is our annual data on firm births. There is another, subtle technical point here: annual data end in March, meaning the data cover the twelve months leading up to March of a given year. So that first jump in the black line means that in the twelve months leading to March 2022, we saw a big jump in actual firm births, not just new Starbuck locations. They jumped in 2022, then moved down a bit in 2023, but stayed elevated. And these firm entrants created nearly two million jobs per year over the last couple of years. That is the highest pace of job creation from new firms since around 2007.

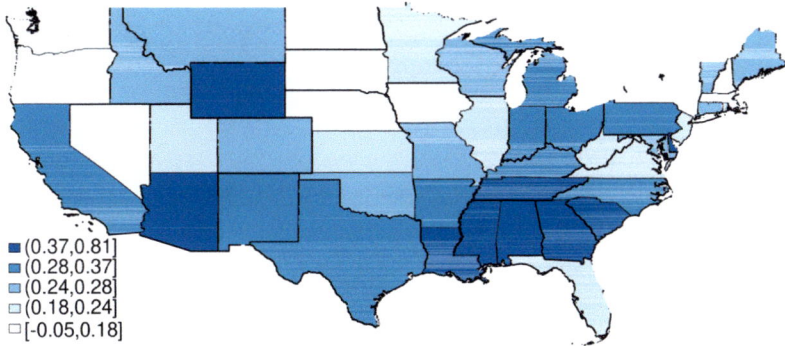

■ (0.37,0.81]
■ (0.28,0.37]
■ (0.24,0.28]
□ (0.18,0.24]
□ [-0.05,0.18]

Note: Difference of average (log) likely employer applications per capita, 2020-2023 vs. 2010-2019.
Source: Census Bureau Business Formation Statistics and population estimates.
See also O'Brien 2022; Newman & O'Brien
2023; Newman & Fikri 2024

Note: State data for likely employer applications; county data for total applications

Let's talk about some pandemic themes, starting with geography. I am going to show how this surge makes sense. Now, I am an economist, and we are often good at explaining things after the fact that we did not see coming. I am going to do that today: take advantage of hindsight. Here is the surge in business applications by state. Let's take the pandemic-pace of business applications and compare it to the pre-pandemic-pace by state. We will take it on a per capita basis, so that we are not just picking up population flows. Which states saw the biggest increase in applications during the pandemic compared to pre-pandemic? There are some familiar patterns here: economic activity moved away from the Northeast towards the South, the Sun Belt, and the West.

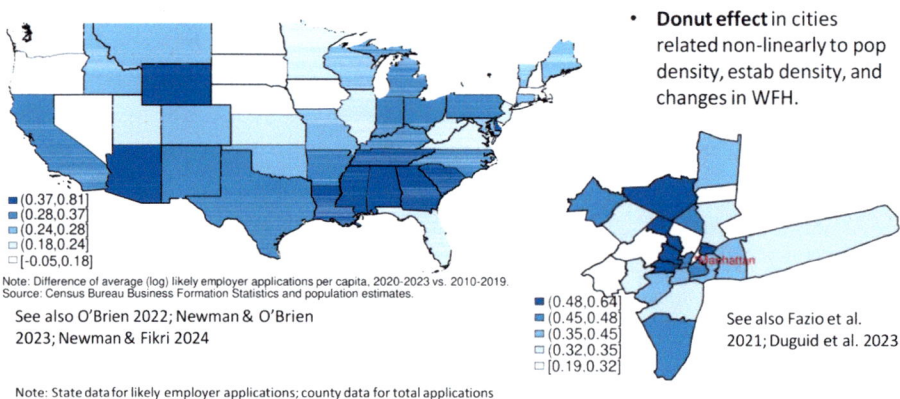

- **Donut effect** in cities related non-linearly to pop density, estab density, and changes in WFH.

Legend (left map):
- (0.37,0.81]
- (0.28,0.37]
- (0.24,0.28]
- (0.18,0.24]
- [-0.05,0.18]

Note: Difference of average (log) likely employer applications per capita, 2020-2023 vs. 2010-2019.
Source: Census Bureau Business Formation Statistics and population estimates.
See also O'Brien 2022; Newman & O'Brien 2023; Newman & Fikri 2024

Legend (right map):
- (0.48,0.64]
- (0.45,0.48]
- (0.35,0.45]
- (0.32,0.35]
- [0.19,0.32]

See also Fazio et al. 2021; Duguid et al. 2023

Note: State data for likely employer applications; county data for total applications

Within cities, there is also an interesting geography story. This map on the right is showing you New York City's counties. If you look at Manhattan, the little white county in the middle, business applications did not surge. Manhattan's new business entry rates have tended historically to be high, so this is a break from the pre-pandemic norm. Our statistical analysis shows that this was generally the pattern in large cities: when compared with the suburbs, application increases in city centers were very low, and these patterns were correlated with remote work activity. This is a familiar pattern: new gyms and restaurants opened in the suburbs probably because more people were working from home. We are all familiar with what has happened in downtown areas, especially in major cities, and more in some parts of the country than in others. This movement from downtown areas to the surrounding counties is consistent with other pandemic stories.

It turns out that we see the same thing in the actual establishment entry as we did for E.I.N. applications. Let's look at the net establishment entry at the county level in all U.S. counties. The chart on the right is a simple scatter plot. The horizontal axis is the surge in applications at the county level (pandemic versus pre-pandemic pace). And the vertical axis is the surge in net establishment entry at the county level. The counties that saw a surge in applications also saw a surge in actual employer establishment

Difference vs pre-pandemic pace (logs)

Slope = .046
S.E. = .005

y-axis: Establishments per capita (0, .05, .1, .15)
x-axis: Business applications per capita (-.5, 0, .5, 1, 1.5)

Note: 2020-2022 vs 2010-2019. County-level binscatter.

(0.12,0.22]
(0.09,0.12]
(0.06,0.09]
(0.04,0.06]
[0.01,0.04]

Note: Difference of average (log) establishments per capita, 2020-2022 vs. 2010-2019.
Source: QCEW and Census Bureau population estimates.

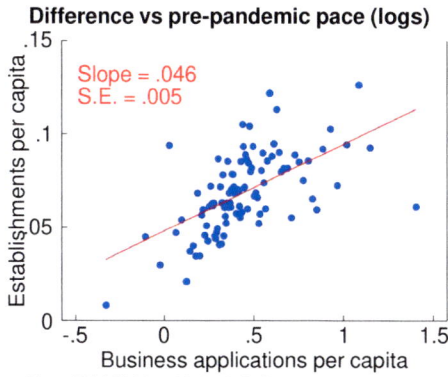

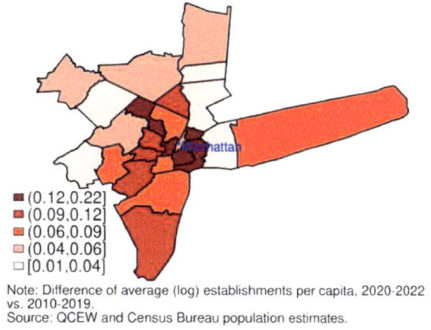

entry. There is a positive, strong correlation between the two. The story is similar in New York City. We find that, in general, the actual employer establishment entry followed a similar pattern within cities.

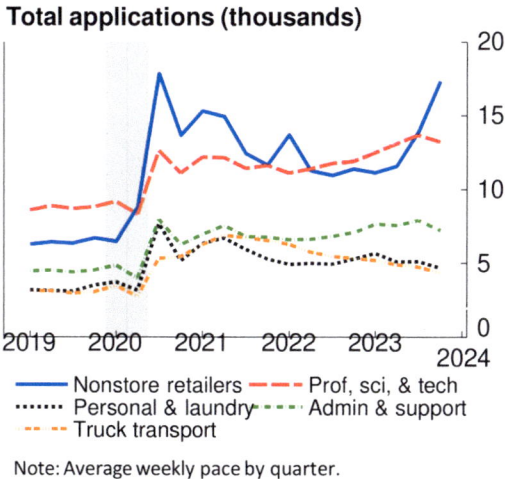

Total applications (thousands)

y-axis: (0, 5, 10, 15, 20)
x-axis: 2019, 2020, 2021, 2022, 2023, 2024

—— Nonstore retailers　　– – – Prof, sci, & tech
········ Personal & laundry　–·–·– Admin & support
– – – Truck transport

Note: Average weekly pace by quarter.

Now we will address some big industry stories during the pandemic. I am going into a relatively narrow level of industry detail. I have identified the top five industries that gave us these applications. The biggest one is the blue line, which shows non-store retail including online retail. There was a huge application surge in online retail during the pandemic. The chart shows a big blip in 2023. That is likely spurious: there were some changes to reporting requirements for marketplace third party sellers. But if you ignore that blip, you see an initial huge surge in non-store, then online retail that has eased off throughout the pandemic.

The red line is professional, scientific, and technical services. This is a large sector that includes industries ranging from home appraisers and architects, to various important high-tech services. It also includes some of the high-tech services that in survey data have been associated with A.I. activities within firms. The red line also includes computer systems design and research and development services. It has had a solid surge, and if anything, it has picked up over the last year or two.

Personal and laundry includes pet care. I'm not sure what exactly is happening in this group of industries, but maybe many people bought pets in 2020. Let's skip to truck transportation, which includes last mile delivery. This makes sense. Early during the pandemic, there was a surge in people having purchases delivered to their houses. That required a lot more delivery vehicles. You can see it rise in 2021-2022, which is when the U.S. had tremendous supply chain challenges, including in freight markets and trucking markets. These industries are conducive to pandemic work, lifestyle, and business. The application surge starts to make sense.

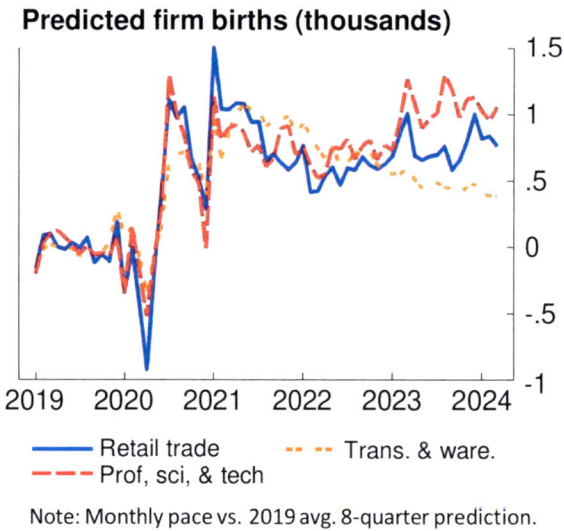

Predicted firm births (thousands)

Legend: Retail trade — Trans. & ware. — Prof, sci, & tech

Note: Monthly pace vs. 2019 avg. 8-quarter prediction.

Let me show another application-based series that uses an actual predictive model. The Census Bureau receives applications and then builds a model that looks at an application's characteristics and predicts whether it will turn into a true employer firm birth. They can do this because they have the data on both sides of the transition. The blue line is retail trade at the broad sector level. That little jump I told you about in 2023 does not show up here, meaning the predictive model was not fooled. Let me highlight the professional scientific and technical services line—the red line—which has been picking up recently. It is still an application-based series. It is predictive of the employer entry, but it is application based.

Difference vs. pre-pandemic pace (logs)

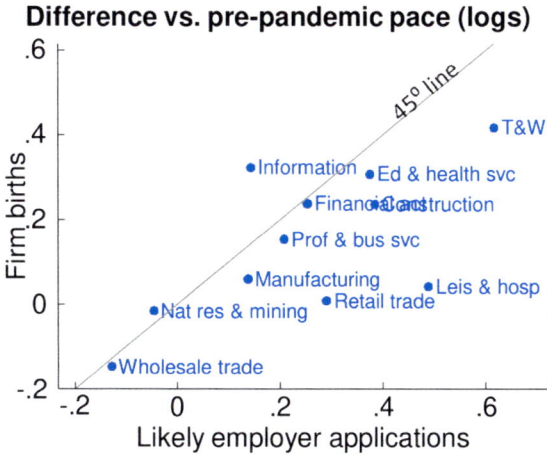

Note: 2021-2023 vs 2011-2020, March reference month.

Here we have some actual employer entry information. This scatterplot compares actual employer entry to the application surge at the broad sector level. The horizontal axis shows the surge in applications. And then I look at the surge in actual firm births. The 45-degree line is growth rates. Sectors that land on that 45-degree line saw the same surge in applications and in firm births. Quite a few sectors are on the line. Sectors that saw a big application surge did in fact see a surge in firm births.

There are a couple of noteworthy exceptions. Retail is the most glaring: the surge in applications in the retail sector was much larger than what actual employer data has shown. There is also an exception in the information sector. That is a tech intensive sector that includes things like software publishing and data hosting. Very interestingly, the fact that we saw a bigger increase in actual firm births than we did in applications might suggest that the transition rates—transitions from application to employer—in that industry were very high. Now we can slice these data a bunch of different ways—we can do it with establishment births or in narrower levels of industry detail. In general, we see that industries with a lot of applications saw a lot of employer entry. Now, let's segue into high tech's role.

There is a long research literature in economics suggesting that business entry, among other sources of dynamism, is historically important for aggregate productivity.

America's last big productivity boom, from the late 90s to the early 2000s, was associated with high tech using and producing sectors that had seen an earlier surge in business entry. So we hope that this pandemic surge in entry is going to lead to stronger U.S. productivity growth going forward. But there might be reasons to be skeptical of that hope.

One possibility is that the business entry surge is a simple restructuring. If we move the restaurants and gyms from the downtown area to the suburbs, the effects on aggregate economy-wide productivity are unlikely to be very substantial. It is great for those entrepreneurs and for the people who want to work from home and have those businesses nearby, but it is probably not going to drive aggregate productivity and G.D.P. much higher. And that kind of entry is part of the story, as the evidence I just showed suggests. But there is an alternative theory: there could have been a burst of innovation.

Net establishment gains (logs; 2019 = 0)

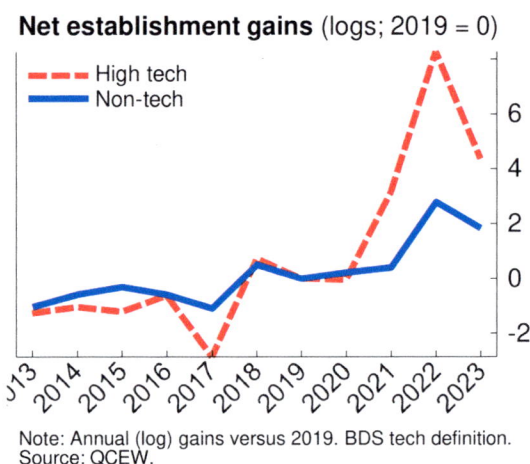

Note: Annual (log) gains versus 2019. BDS tech definition.
Source: QCEW.

Let's investigate the industry composition of the surge in employer establishment entry. I am going to focus on narrower industry detail where we can think about how high-tech intensive a specific narrow industry is and what kind of establishment entry patterns we saw in those industries. This chart shows annual net establishment gains in growth rates. The horizontal axis represents percentage points, roughly speaking. It is normalized to 2019, so 2019 is zero. And you can see this surge relative to the pre-pandemic pace.

I've divided these narrow industries into high-tech or non-tech. In this case, we are looking at how STEM intensive this industry's employment is. Is this an industry that employs a lot of high-tech type people? If it is, we will call them tech. These high-tech industries saw an enormous increase in net establishment creation during the pandemic. In 2022, the net establishment entry rate was about eight percentage points higher than the pre-pandemic norm. And the pre-pandemic norm for high-tech was something like four percent a year. It is quite striking. Now, if I had shown you this chart without the tech line and only the blue line—the non-tech industries—you would have found that striking too. In fact, we have seen a large increase in establishment formation in non-tech industries as well. But the tech surge is much larger.

Rank		Industry	Change (1000s)
1	5415	Computer Systems Design and Related Services	120
2	5416	Management, Scientific, and Technical Consulting Services	114
4	5112	Software Publishers	53
13	5413	Architectural, Engineering, and Related Services	27
15	5182	Data Processing, Hosting, and Related Services	26
17	5511	Management of Companies and Enterprises	24
19	5417	Scientific Research and Development Services	22

Note: Top 20 4-digit NAICS industries by establishment change (1000s), 2019 to 2023. Tech defined by BDS-HT definitions or Hecker (2005).
Source: QCEW.

Note: Aggregate establishment gain = 1.7 million

So there does seem to be something here. We have pushed on this question and found the result to be pretty robust. I made a list of the top twenty narrow industries in terms of the number of establishments that they gained since the pandemic started. I have also listed the four-digit industry codes. Tech is a relatively small share of the economy, depending how you define it, only about five to fifteen percent, but it is overrepresented among the top twenty industries.

Here are the tech industries that fall within the top twenty industries for pandemic net establishment entry. There are some interesting industries here, including computer systems design and related services. There are many reasons one might need such services, not only to help companies transition to work from home, but also A.I. investment requires an enormous amount of computer system design. There's also technical consulting, software publishers, and research and development services.

There is another important bit of technical detail you need to know: industry codes are set at the establishment level. Walmart is a retailer. But if Walmart opens a data center somewhere, it will register in the data in the appropriate industry category, such as a data center type industry. The scientific research and development services could be any number of services attached to incumbent firms. The establishment births here could be incumbent firms or new firms. But these numbers are striking. Computer systems design added 120,000 establishments since the pandemic started. That is enormous; the total increase in establishments is about 1.7 million, and 120,000 of them are coming from that one little industry. Now, you might say this is a little unfair to the tiny industries. If you are a small but important industry, you cannot add that many establishments and get high in this ranking.

So let's do it another way and just look at the industry level growth rate in the number of establishments. And we get a similar list here that ends up reordered a bit. Scientific R&D comes in a bit higher; it is the sixth highest industry in terms of its within-industry growth. The number of establishments in the software publishers industry more than doubled during the pandemic. You even see some manufacturing. There is some very important, high-tech activity in the manufacturing sector we see here. The tech story seems legitimate.

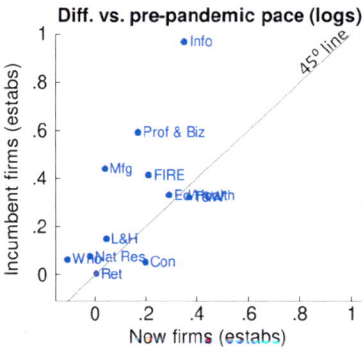

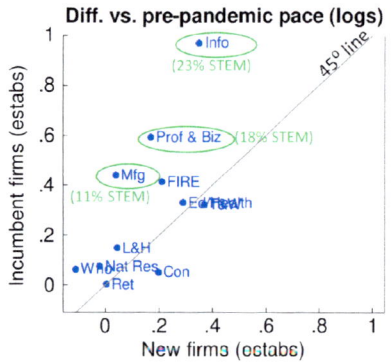

But we do not know yet whether existing firms or entrepreneurs are opening these new tech sector establishments. We do not have the data yet, so I cannot answer this exactly, but I can get close. First, at the broad sector level, I can look at establishment births, and I can separate incumbent firm establishment births from entirely new firms. If Walmart opens a data center, for example, that is an incumbent firm establishment birth, and I can separate that from the genuine new firms. I am going to do it in growth terms relative to pre-pandemic. On the horizontal axis, I am looking at the growth in establishment births coming from new firms. And on the vertical axis, I am doing it for incumbent firms. If you are on the 45-degree line, you are a sector that saw the same increase in establishment births from both new firms and incumbents. If you are above the 45-degree line, incumbents played a larger role. And you can see there are some some sectors that are above the line. In green in particular, some are particularly tech intensive—the information sector, professional and business services, and manufacturing. These industries all have relatively high STEM shares. In fact, these are the top three industries, depending what year you measure it. Each of these saw bigger surge in establishment births from incumbent firms than from new firms. Let me emphasize that a couple of these did get a significant increase from new firms as well. If you look at the information sector, it is well along that horizontal axis, as is the professional and business sector. Manufacturing is not. So it seems like both new firms and incumbent firms are participating in this tech establishment entry story, though more on the incumbent side than on the new firm side.

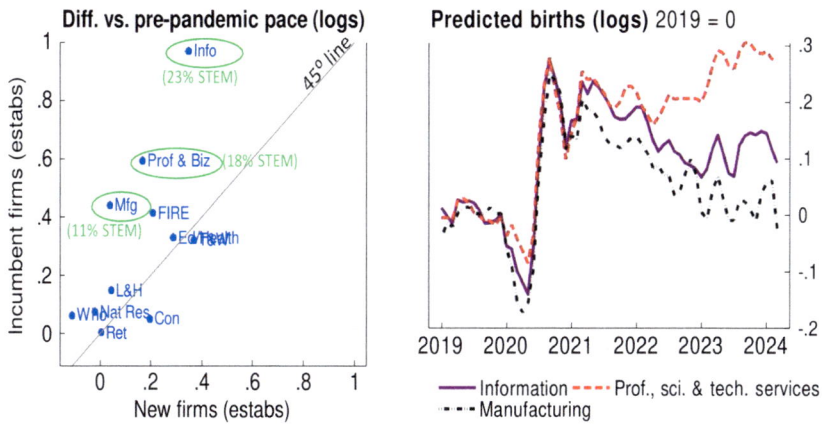

But let's note one other thing: if we think back to that application data from earlier, I told you how the Census Bureau has internal modeling that predicts actual firm births and that these predictions tend to be accurate using the application data. I have their predicted firm births from the application data here for these three big tech sectors. It looks like early in the pandemic, there were a lot of predicted births in manufacturing, but it has eased off. But the professional, scientific, and technical services prediction is still high and indeed it has picked up recently. And again, this is an important sector. It includes a lot of important high-tech services, such as research and development, computer systems design, etc.

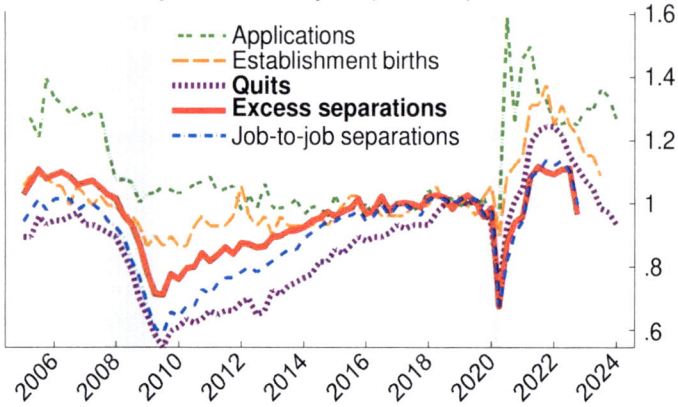

Business entry and worker quits (2019 = 1)

- - - Applications
- - - Establishment births
.... **Quits**
Excess separations
- - - Job-to-job separations

Let's shift gears and talk about one more pandemic item before turning to longer run trends. You might remember hearing the term "great resignation." During the pandemic and in the years following the pandemic, we saw an incredible increase in the share of workers quitting their jobs in a given month. This chart's purple dotted line shows the quit rate—the monthly share of workers who quit their jobs. If you look at the pandemic period, you can see the great resignation in the data. It was very elevated in 2021 and 2022. The green line is the likely employer application series from the beginning of my talk. And the orange line is the establishment birth series. Establishment births and quits move together closely. There are obvious theories for why this might be the case: people quit their jobs and flowed to these new establishments, for example, either as early workers or potentially as firm founders. But it is also the case that there are a lot of macroeconomic time series that behave similarly during the pandemic. It was an extreme event; we should not draw too many conclusions from just looking at these lines.

So what I want to do is go down to fine geographic detail. I cannot do that in the quits data because it is not available at the county level, but I can with a proxy called excess separations. To calculate total separations, we look at all the workers who left their firms for any number of reasons over a given period. We are going to calculate excess separations by subtracting off what economists call job destruction. If you leave your firm, and your firm never refills your job, the firm's total head count decreases. That is job destruction. If that happens, it is reasonable to assume your firm laid you off; the firm's size decreased. If you leave your firm but someone else immediately replaces you and the firm does not destroy the job, then that often represents a quit. Firing is also possible, but quits are much more common.

Difference vs pre-pandemic pace (logs)

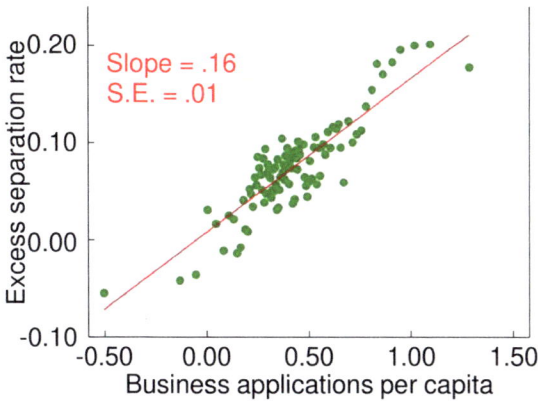

Note: 2020-2022 vs 2010-2019. County-level binscatter.

Excess separations are used as a proxy for quits historically and in economic research. The separations in which you were immediately replaced move closely with what economists call job-to-job separations. That is the chart's blue line. If the worker immediately went to another job, that is likely a quit. At the county level, I can use excess separations as a proxy for quits. What I want to see is if this pandemic-era seeming relationship between business entry and quits holds up across geography and is not just a spurious time series aggregation issue.

This scatterplot uses county level data. Business applications per capita—the surge in business applications relative to pre-pandemic—is plotted on the horizontal axis. I can do this for other measures like establishment entry and get a similar result. The vertical axis is the surge in quits using my proxy of excess separations. What we see is that counties with a high number of business applications also had a lot of quits. To some extent, the great resignation happened in the same counties that this business entry surge happened. This lends some support to the theory that people were quitting their jobs and flowing to these businesses.

I can also calculate this for layoffs. One theory explaining the surge in entry is that if the labor market collapses, people have little choice but to turn to self-employment. The pace of layoffs surged in 2020. The labor market was bad for a time. But that does not explain the business entry surge that we also got. So, if I make this same scatterplot using layoffs or job destruction, we see a very, very weak relationship. Depending on how I specify it, the relationship is negative, zero, or slightly positive, but nothing like what we are seeing here. Layoffs were high in 2020 and parts of 2021, but the layoff pace in aggregate has been very subdued for the last couple of years. So the idea that layoffs are causing the surge and entry is not consistent with the fact that layoffs decreased far earlier than the entry surge. It would seem the great resignation is partly related to this business surge in entry. Entry seems to have played some role in this enormous churning of workers that we have seen over the last three years.

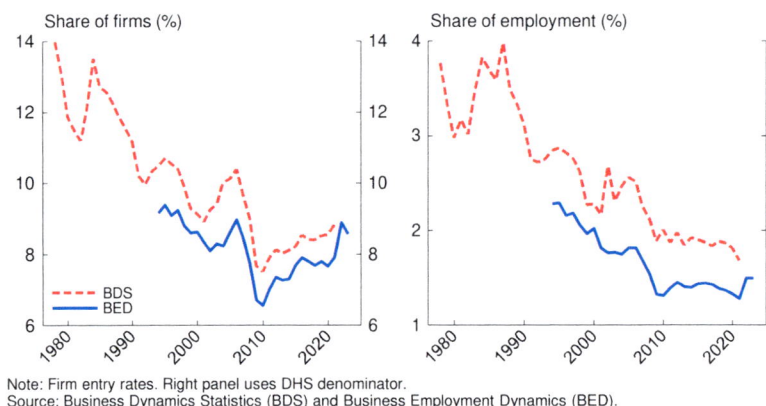

Note: Firm entry rates. Right panel uses DHS denominator.
Source: Business Dynamics Statistics (BDS) and Business Employment Dynamics (BED).

Now we will turn to some pre-pandemic trends. Part of what made this surge so remarkable and surprising is that prior to the pandemic, the U.S. had seen a multi-decade decline in business entry rates. The chart shows this in a couple of ways. On the chart's left is the entry rate—the number of new firms divided by the total number of firms. New firms as a share of all firms has had a long run trend decline. On the right panel, I show business entry rates as share of employment: jobs that new firms create as a share of all the economy's jobs. That has also been declining. As the chart shows, these are some large declines. In the economics literature, this is called the secular decline in business dynamism. The literature is extensive. I have a paper with my current co-author and others from 2014, in which we documented a lot of these trends.[2]

Other dynamism measures were declining as well during this time period. Job reallocation—the pace at which jobs are reallocated across the economy—was declining. Businesses shrink and grow and jobs flow between them. The pace of worker reallocation—quits and hires and the rate at which workers are switching jobs—had also been declining. Even rates of internal U.S. migration had been declining.

There had also been a trend of weaker productivity selection. An important element of a market economy is that productive businesses—the ones with the good ideas—need to

The Austin Symposium

grow. They are the ones that need the workers and the capital. Unproductive businesses need to shrink or exit. Productivity selection has been an important contributor to aggregate productivity growth in the past, and it had weakened pre-pandemic. It was still there, and the relationship was still positive at the firm or establishment level, but it had been slowing down. The trends also pointed to rising average firm size and concentration. The decline in measures of dynamism could have big implications for aggregate job creation. There's even evidence that some of the productivity growth slowdown we saw after 2004 might have been related to this decline in dynamism. It even matters for business cycles.

The literature on this is large and explaining this decline was occupying an enormous amount of time. We have not nailed its exact cause. The literature proposes various theories; one is demographics. Historically, and even in standard economic models, business entrants absorb labor force growth. Without labor force growth, it is hard for businesses to enter. The U.S. did see slowing labor force growth pre-pandemic. That might be part of the story. There are also stories about the regulatory and business policy environment: a tax on firing is a tax on hiring. There is some evidence that unlawful discharge regulations and the like may have slowed down dynamism.

There are also possible benign causes for the decline in dynamism. We wrote a paper in which we argued that part of the decline was concentrated in the retail trade sector, where we saw the rise of big box retail. It turns out that big box retail is enormously productive, much more productive than the businesses that they replaced. And they pay better wages. But that did not explain all of it.

There are other stories as well. It is popular recently to talk about rising market power and the idea that the U.S. economy is becoming monopolized. Researchers have tried to calculate market power measures and argue that it is related to declining entry. I'm pretty skeptical. Brian Albrecht and I have a recent paper that looks at industries and we do not find that result. But it is a popular story. There are also stories about knowledge investment. Does the increasing importance of knowledge-based capital, as opposed to physical capital, in the productive process create difficulties for new firms and slow down the diffusion of ideas?

So now the question is, did the pandemic surge end the decline? Are we reversing that trend? It is still too early to tell. The blue line in the chart on declining entry rates shows the last couple of years of firm entry rates. Those are pretty striking jumps

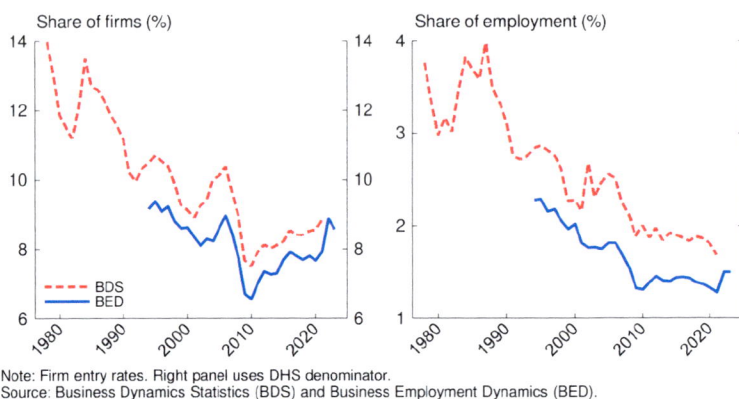

Note: Firm entry rates. Right panel uses DHS denominator.
Source: Business Dynamics Statistics (BDS) and Business Employment Dynamics (BED).

relative to historic trends, but they do not get us anywhere near to where we were in the 80s or the 90s in terms of firm entry rates. So that is the first issue: this rebound is small compared to the longer run trend. Additionally, some of our papers show that these pandemic-era entrants have been a little smaller than entrants pre-pandemic. That could suggest that these businesses are going to have a lower survival rate or might not have past entrants' high quality.

The chart does not show it, but I could show you job reallocation. That is another dynamism story. It is similar to entry in that there was a big jump in job reallocation during the pandemic, but even with that jump we are nowhere close to the 90s-era entry rate. More generally, to get a durable reversal of the pre-pandemic trends, we need continued surging entry. Most importantly, we need those recent entrants to grow; they need to innovate, grow, and survive. It is too early to tell what their fates will be, but it is worth keeping in mind.

The other thing to keep in mind are the theories that explain the pre-pandemic decline. Pick a theory you believe is true and then ask, is that still true? If the demographic headwinds are still there, the business and policy environments have not changed, and all these elements are the same, you would not expect the trend to suddenly reverse and bring us back to where we were decades ago. So I think we will still have to think about these longer run stories.

What happened in the pandemic was a remarkable, unexpected story. At the very beginning of the pandemic, applications dipped for a couple of months. Many people predicted that the pandemic would cause a complete collapse of business entry and that was going to have knock on effects on labor markets for years to come. There was a lot of concern during those first couple months. And then we have this enormous reversal. It is quite a story.

But entrepreneurs did what entrepreneurs do; they saw opportunities and they went after them. There were massive changes to consumption, work, lifestyle, and business patterns. Many businesses needed to build out their IT infrastructure, so that they could facilitate work from home or online retail. These were opportunities and entrepreneurs did what they do, which is go after these opportunities. It is an incredible story and a testament to American dynamism. Despite these longer run trends, American dynamism is really something to behold. And the best we can tell in cross-country comparisons, other countries have not seen this. Some countries have seen some growth in entry, but none have seen what we have seen here. It is a remarkable story. Counting out the American entrepreneur was a mistake.

The entry surge seems to have facilitated or followed the broader pandemic economic restructuring across geography and industry. It might be an important ingredient of the remarkable post-pandemic labor market recovery and some of these other reallocations that had to happen. We do have evidence that high tech industries saw a large and disproportionate entry surge. Some of that might be early pandemic stories about online retail and work from home. But it increasingly looks like it could be related to other stories around big IT investments for things like A.I. And then it seems possible that many quitters flowed to the new businesses. So, we have seen some shifts in the industry and geographic pattern of economic activity, and we have a slightly younger firm age distribution. That is the first time in a long time that has happened, a little bit more activity at small firms, and a pause in pre-pandemic trends.

Endnotes

[1] See Decker, Ryan and John Haltiwanger (2024), "Surging business formation in the pandemic: Causes and consequences?" Brookings Papers on Economic Activity, Fall 2023; Decker, Ryan and John Haltiwanger (2024), "High tech business entry in the pandemic era," FEDS Notes, 29 April, at https://doi.org/10.17016/2380-7172.3499; and Decker, Ryan and John Haltiwanger (2024), "Surging business formation in the pandemic: A brief update," working paper, at https://rdeckernet.github.io/website/DH_businessformation_update.pdf.

[2] Decker, Ryan, John Haltiwanger, Ron Jarmin, and Javier Miranda (2014), "The role of entrepreneurship in U.S. job creation and economic dynamism," Journal of Economic Perspectives 28:3-24.

6. The Housing and Migration Crisis

Daniel Shoag

There is a Jewish teaching that warns against lecturing people who are wiser, cleverer, more knowledgeable, or smarter than you are, because you could embarrass yourself. I usually joke that when I stand up to lecture, I pause and somberly assess the room before concluding that it is not a problem. But not today; the Austin Symposium's speakers—Deirdre McCloskey, Ryan Decker, Ed Glaeser, Ned Phelps, and Cass Sunstein—have been fantastic.

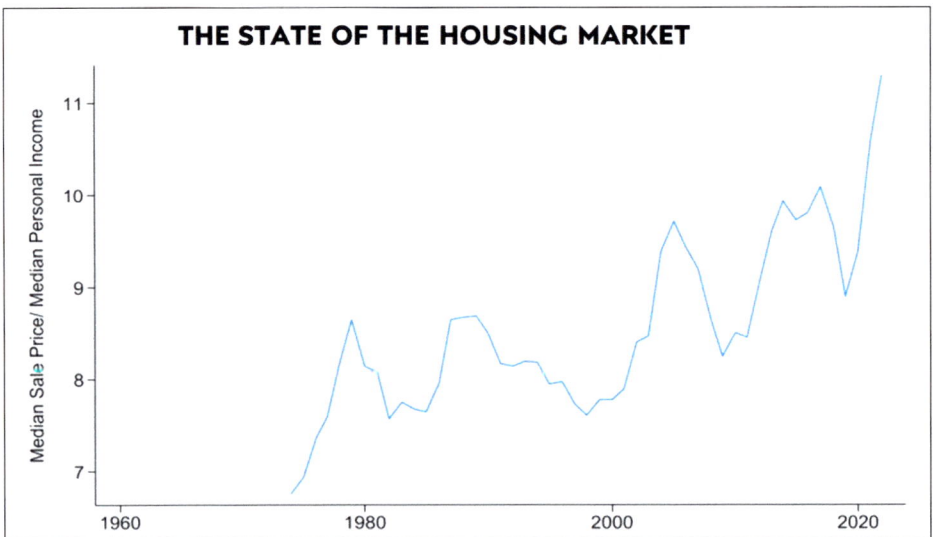

THE STATE OF THE HOUSING MARKET

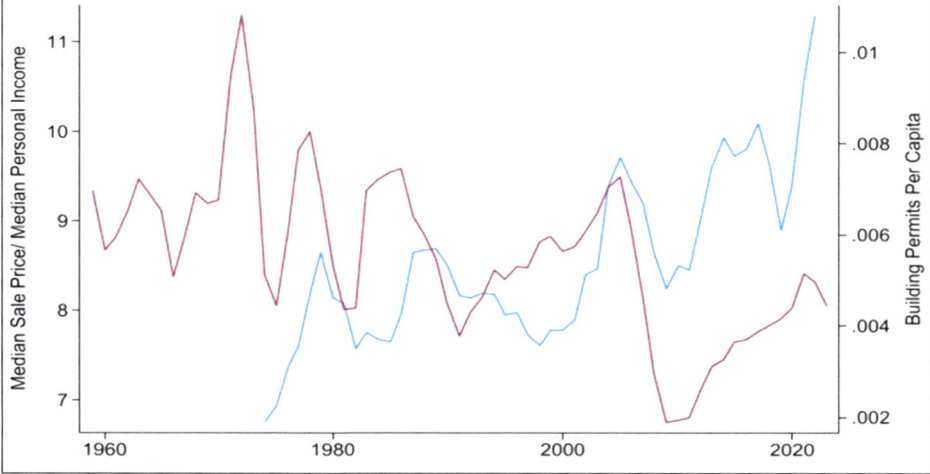

THE STATE OF THE HOUSING MARKET

Let us talk about the state of the housing market and its regulatory problems, starting with the problem. In terms of house prices relative to income and/or affordability measures, the U.S. is close to an all-time high, though recent months have seen a slight reduction. Looking at the latest data, the median house price is around $420,000. That is high. If you use conventional benchmarks for what the average household can afford, the median house is too expensive for around seventy percent of households.

Home prices are becoming genuinely unaffordable. One would assume we would increase construction to increase supply and lower the cost, but that is not happening. If you look at permits per capita, represented on the chart's red line. It is relatively low—not as low as the recent historical bottom in the 2008 recession, but low per capita relative to historic patterns. Why are prices so high? Why aren't we building at the rate that we used to or that we should build to keep up with demand?

WHAT IS GOING ON?

Index Value (y-axis): 0, 200, 400, 600

Lines labeled: House Prices, Construction Labor, Construction Materials PPI

x-axis: 1970, 1980, 1990, 2000, 2010, 2020

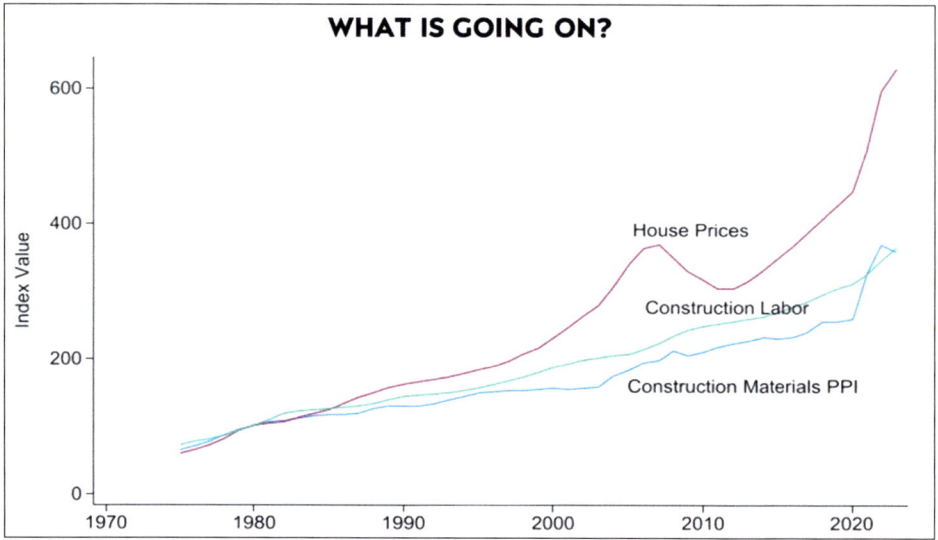

If housing prices seem high, we should compare them against relative input costs, using an index of construction labor and construction materials. Those inputs are certainly more expensive overall now than they were in the past, but not expensive enough to explain housing prices. We can think of the gap between house prices and how they have grown relative to materials or labor as a regulatory tax.

Affordability problems are multi-dimensional. Conventional wisdom explains them through many myths. One big myth claims that some fundamental market failure independent of regulations caused the skyrocketing prices. But the lack of supply is testament to the regulations, not some fundamental inability to build. Another myth you often hear is that you are talking about luxury housing or market rate construction, but these factors do not really affect affordability.

This is from a paper by Evan Mast. It shows the process called filtering—the process by which new construction filters down the demand chain. What is happening here? The red dots are newly built units. But the people who move into those units moved from somewhere else and someone new moves into the homes that they vacated, and so on. Building one hundred market rate housing units leads to approximately forty-five to seventy people moving out of below median income homes. Importantly, Mast did not calculate these numbers from statistics; he tracked person by person moving around in the

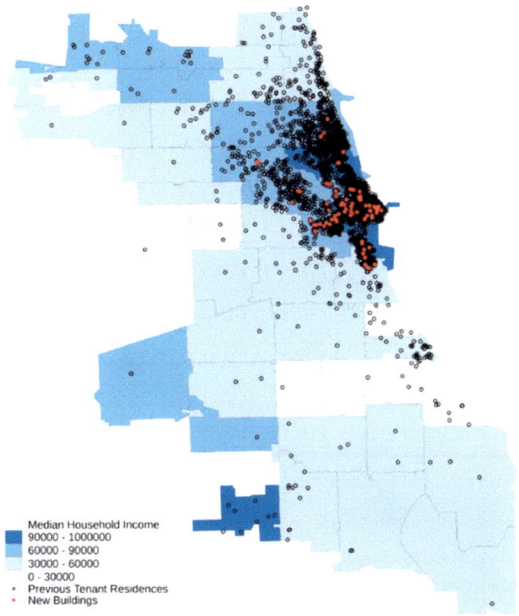

COMMON MYTHS

Median Household Income
- 90000 - 1000000
- 60000 - 90000
- 30000 - 60000
- 0 - 30000
- Previous Tenant Residences
- New Buildings

Chicago area. He tracked people moving around quickly—they are making about three moves within three years.

Perhaps more generous demand subsidies would solve the problem. Maybe we will not need supply increases if we just increase demand. If supply, however, is inelastic, increasing demand will not significantly increase quantity. Studies from Peter Ganong and Rob Collison have looked at increasing the generosity of vouchers and other programs. A great deal of those increases translates into higher prices, not greater quantity. Maybe government subsidies, like LIHTC and tax credits to build low-income housing would help. Stuart Rosenthal's papers show that subsidies usually just crowd out non-subsidized, low-income housing production without significantly increasing quantity.

Maybe housing's inflated cost is due to Airbnb, institutional investors, or foreign buyers. There's research on all these explanations, but when you examine the data, they really do not track. Paper after paper show that regulations restrict supply.

CHANGING REGULATIONS

After 2010:

- **U-SU-C1:** Urban Single Unit (ADU allowed but no duplex, Minimum Zone Lot Size: 5,500 sq. ft.)
- **U-TU-C:** Urban Two Unit (Minimum Zone Lot Size: 5,500 sq. ft.)
- **U-MX-3:** Urban Mixed Use (Maximum Height: 3 Stories)

U-SU-C1 · U-TU-C · U-MX-3 · U-N

CHANGING REGULATIONS

The neighborhood in 2002

4450 Utica St

From Tobias Peters, Ed Pinto, and Hanlu Zhang

This is a paper from Ed Pinto and Tobias Peters looking at a neighborhood north of Denver. In 2010, Denver did some big up-zoning. The city took a neighborhood and kept this orange box as single-family, single units. The pink box they zoned for duplexes. This is a growing area. The green box they zoned for townhouses, which are zoned for a max of three stories. The city turned single family homes into duplexes and townhouses. What happened? If you take this box, where nothing changed, there were about one-hundred units before they did the up-zoning and then one-hundred units after. When you take the box zoned for duplexes, it went from eighty to ninety units and if you take the zone that allowed townhouses, it went from about fifteen to sixty units. We want to increase supply and the constraints on increasing supply in these high productivity, high price areas are coming from zoning.

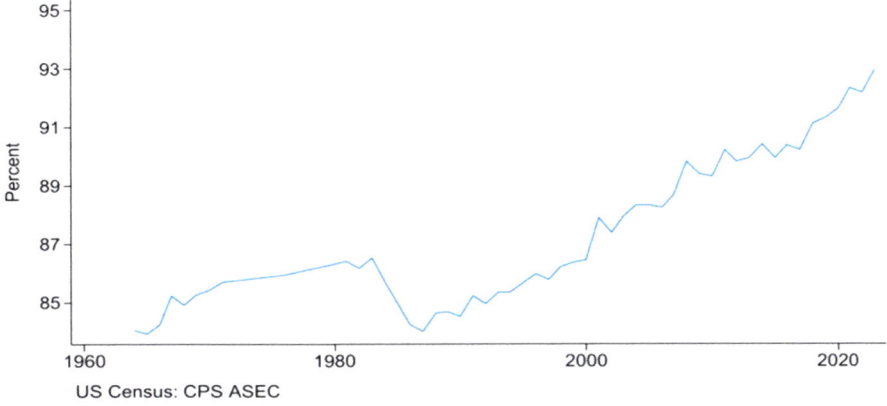

DYNAMISM AND HOUSING

Living in the Same House as Last Year

Ages 25-75

US Census: CPS ASEC

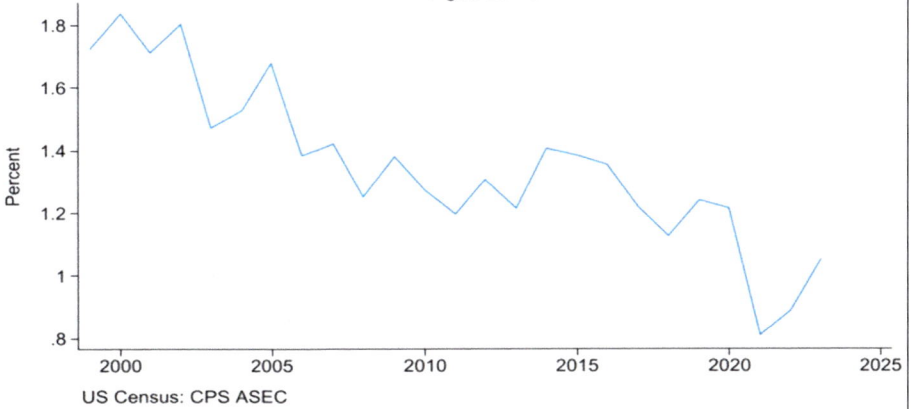

DYNAMISM AND HOUSING

Percent Moving for Work

Ages 25-75

US Census: CPS ASEC

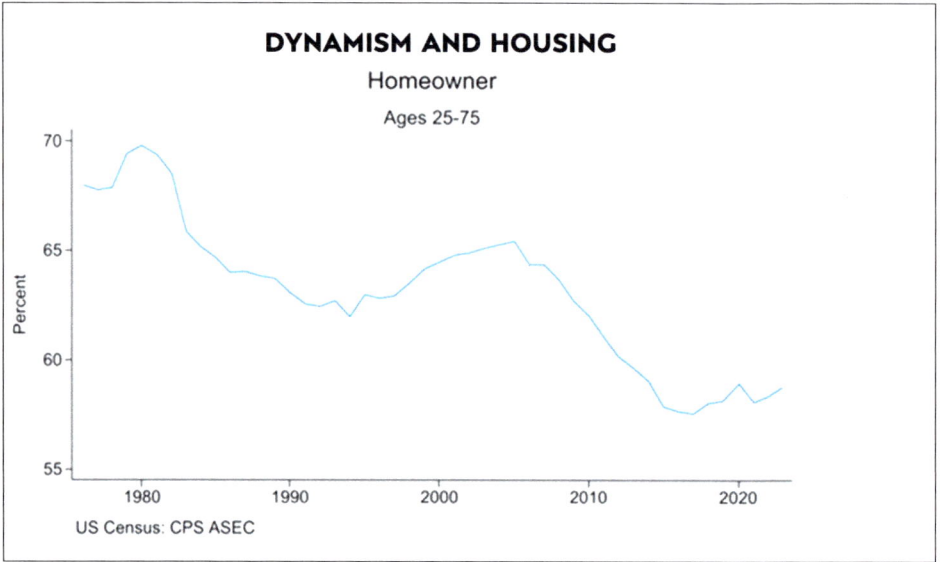

DYNAMISM AND HOUSING

Homeowner

Ages 25-75

US Census: CPS ASEC

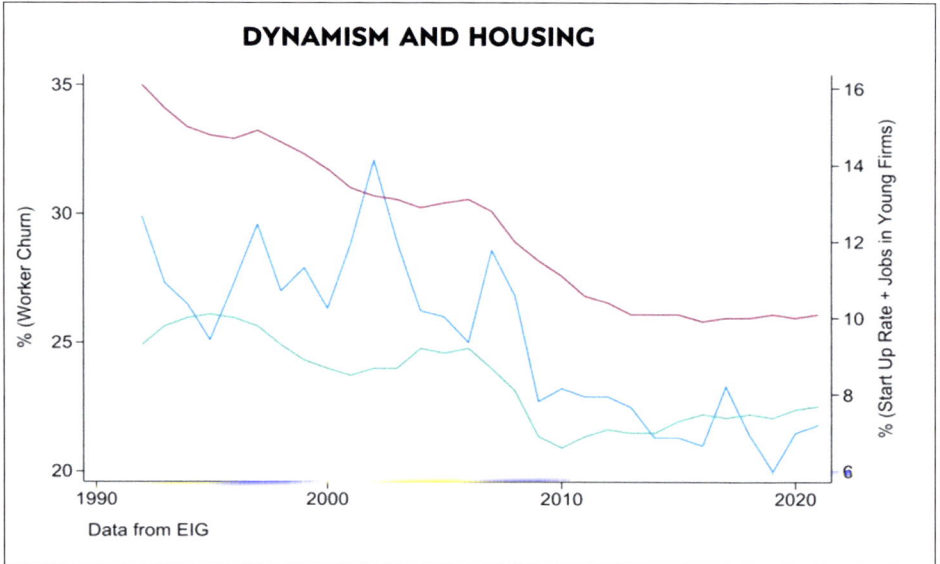

DYNAMISM AND HOUSING

Data from EIG

There are many relationships between these regulatory constraints and dynamism. One we see is that people are less likely to move. There are several ways to measure how people move. One way is to take the opposite approach—how many people have not moved and are living in the same house year after year? How many people are moving for work? The Terner Center Project asks people what caused them to move and three of the explanations offered for them to choose from are work related. The number of people who have not moved over the past year has also been decreasing year after year. People are less likely to be homeowners or to be heads of households. There have been large increases in the number of adults who are living with their parents, for example.

The E.I.G. has has many measures of dynamism, including worker churn, startup rates, percentage of people who work in young firms, and growth in the number of firms. All those measures have declined in the data through 2021. These measures are all correlated at the state level. If we run the correlations between permitting in each of these measures, they show well over sixty percent, which is high for just fifty data points. Other factors also correlate with expensive housing markets or supply restrictions. Enrico Moretti has a paper about misallocation and reductions in G.D.P. Ed Glaeser has done a lot of research about driving's effect on climate; when housing is restricted, people must live farther away from their workplace. Carbon emissions are the result. Even obesity is linked. Several papers link expensive housing to marriage, both declines in the rate of marriage and increase in people staying married because it is harder to get divorced. I also have a paper looking at the relationship between this and fertility.

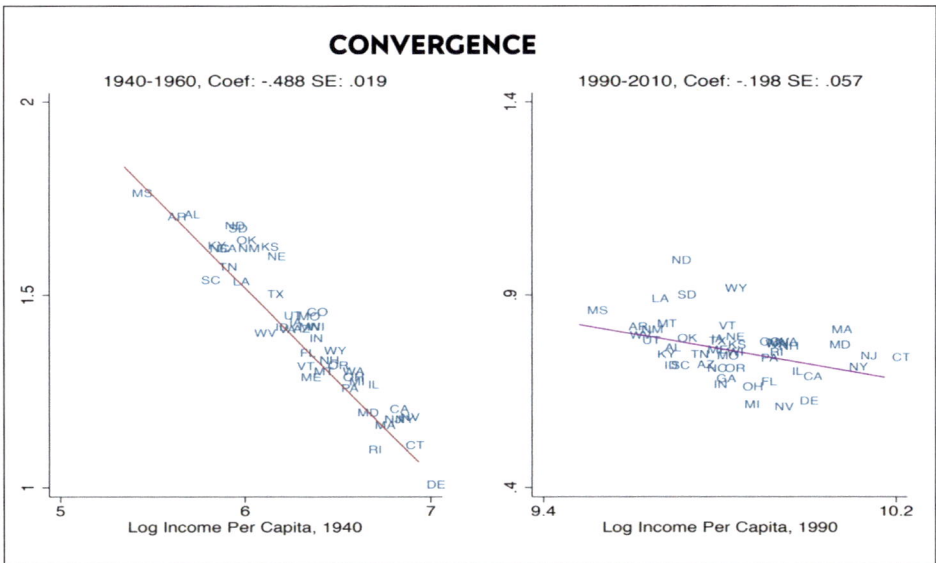

CONVERGENCE

1940-1960, Coef: -.488 SE: .019   1990-2010, Coef: -.198 SE: .057

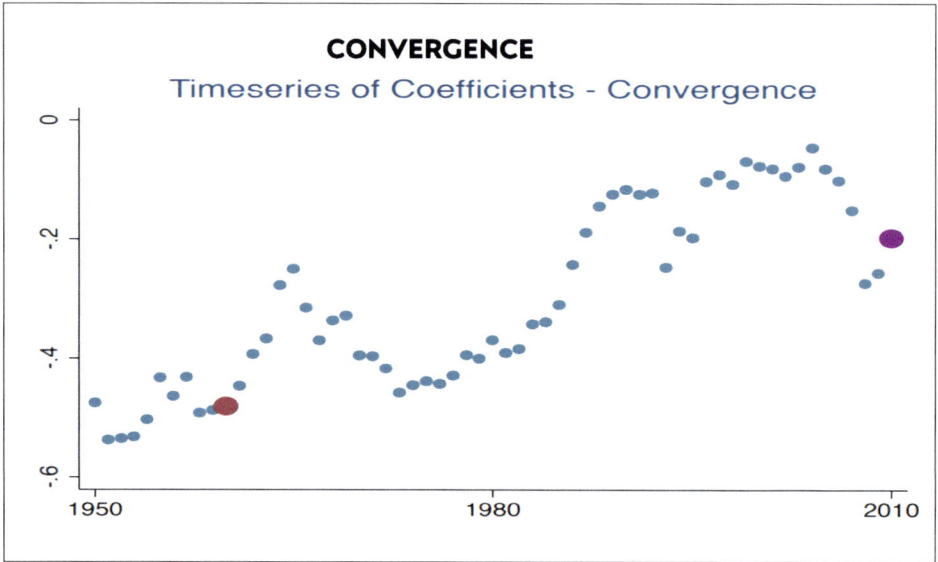

CONVERGENCE
Timeseries of Coefficients - Convergence

Now we will relate regulations that restrict housing supply to an important dimension: dynamism that applies not just locally, but to the general macro economy. Here is a relationship called convergence. On this slide, I have plotted income per capita starting over a twenty-year period from 1940 to 1960. Over here on the right are the rich states, including Connecticut and Delaware. And the lower income states are on the left, Alabama, South Carolina, and so forth. On the y-axis, I have plotted growth, meaning how quickly incomes are growing.

You can see that growth is high across the board. The richer states are growing more slowly than lower income states: the lower income states are growing faster in terms of income per capita. What does that mean? The lower income states started off behind and now they are catching up—converging—with richer states.

This is over twenty years, but we have data all the way back to 1880. If you looked from 1880-1980, you would see this relationship. This is a very good relationship for a non-tautological relationship. Across state relationships, the R-squared is 0.95, which means even if you took handfuls of states, you would still see the same relationship.

In more recent periods, however, the relationship is has mostly disappeared. Not only is the slope much weaker, catch up among states has decreased. On this slide, where you can see growth rates and income per capita, the rich states are on the right and the lower income states on the left. It shows a bit of a negative relationship, but it is still

The Austin Symposium

possible to find a rich state like Massachusetts and a lower income state like Wyoming that are growing at about the same rate, but the R-squared is lower. The catch up speed is just much slower than it was in the past.

These years are not cherry picked. I have plotted this steep slope in red and this weaker slope in pink. I can do this for each twenty-year window. Here is the steep slope, which is sharply negative for 1940-1960. And here is the much weaker pink slope that I estimated more recently. There is a period where these catch-up slopes were large. Then in more recent periods that slope has gotten much weaker.

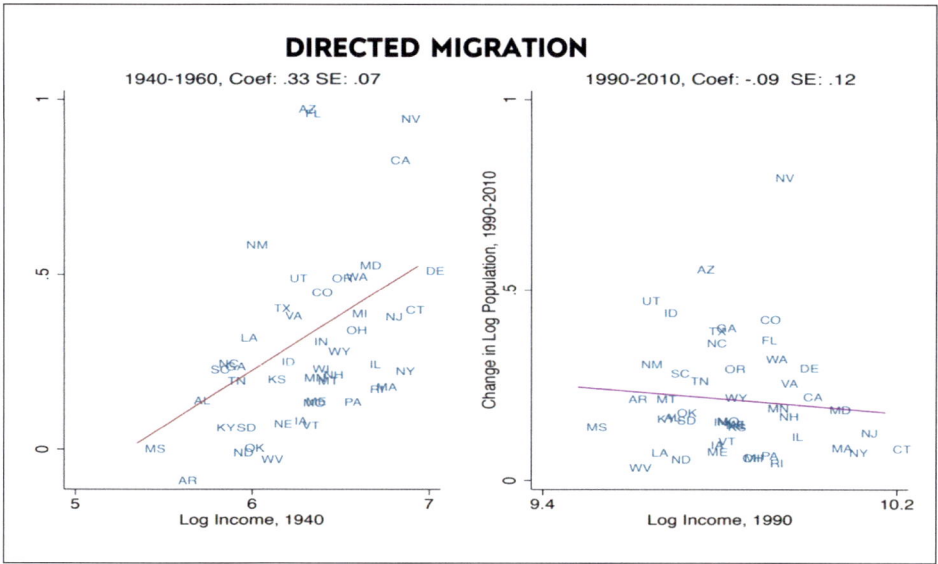

DIRECTED MIGRATION

1940-1960, Coef: .33 SE: .07   1990-2010, Coef: -.09 SE: .12

That is not the only relationship. Here, the x-axis is the same as before. Again, we are looking at the rich states on the right, and the lower income states on the left, but now instead of plotting growth rates in income, I am plotting growth rates in population. I call this relationship directed migration. What we see that a handful of states are growing very quickly in terms of population in 1940-1960. But even in states like Delaware, Maryland, Connecticut, and Michigan, which have relatively high incomes, their population is growing faster than the lower income states; people are moving to states that have the highest incomes during this period.

Now, if we look at a more recent period that relationship is almost gone. Looking at these past graphs, one wonders why they showed income growing the fastest in lower income states. That does not seem to correlate with our recent experience. If we think, moreover, about the parts of the country that are currently growing the fastest, we do not assume that they are these rich states on the graph's right side, because that no longer holds. The richest states are not growing the fastest. Let us look now at not just for these twenty-year windows, but for all twenty-year windows. We will take this red slope and this pink slope and show the relationship over time.

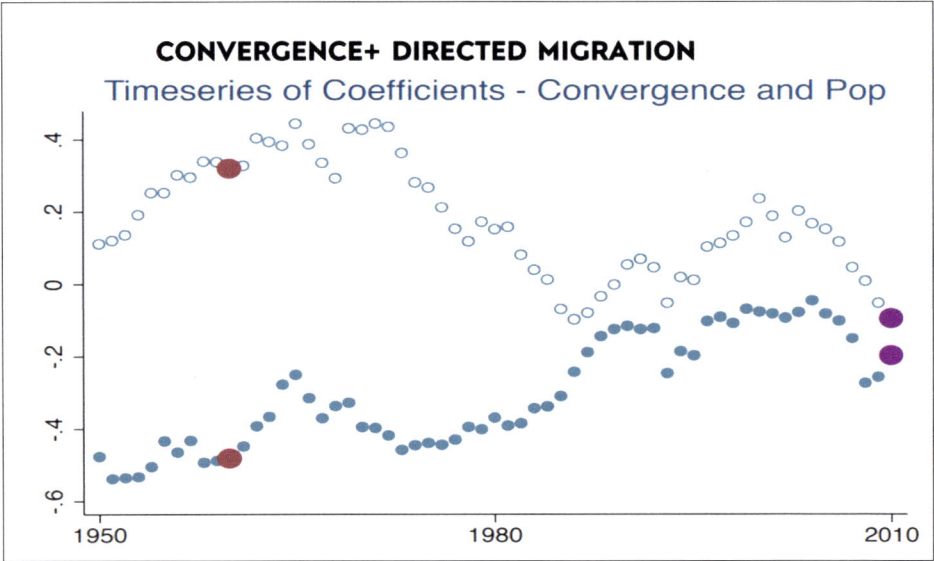

CONVERGENCE+ DIRECTED MIGRATION
Timeseries of Coefficients - Convergence and Pop

This is directed migration where people are moving to the richest parts of the country. Here is where we were in the more recent period where that is not happening. We have divided postwar U.S. history into two periods: a period where people are moving to the richest parts of the country, convergence happens, and the poor states catch up to the rich states. Then in the more recent period, both of those trends slow, or even disappear. And the question is, why? This paper links these trends to a change in the way we build or the change in housing prices and regulations.

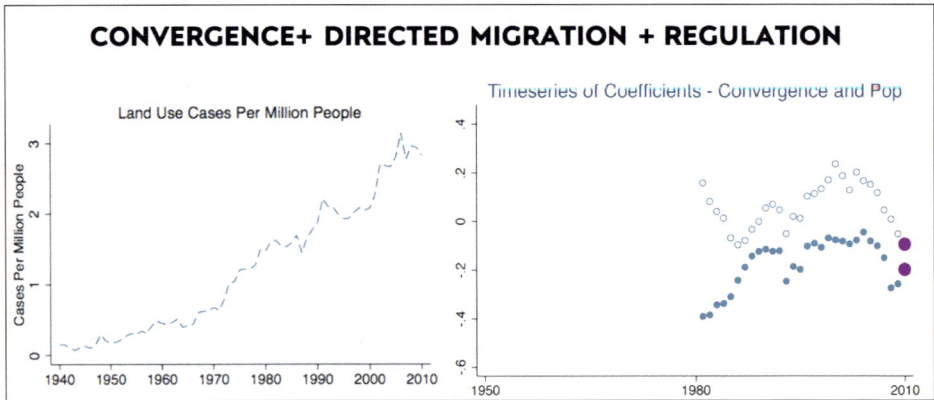

CONVERGENCE+ DIRECTED MIGRATION + REGULATION

Land Use Cases Per Million People

Timeseries of Coefficients - Convergence and Pop

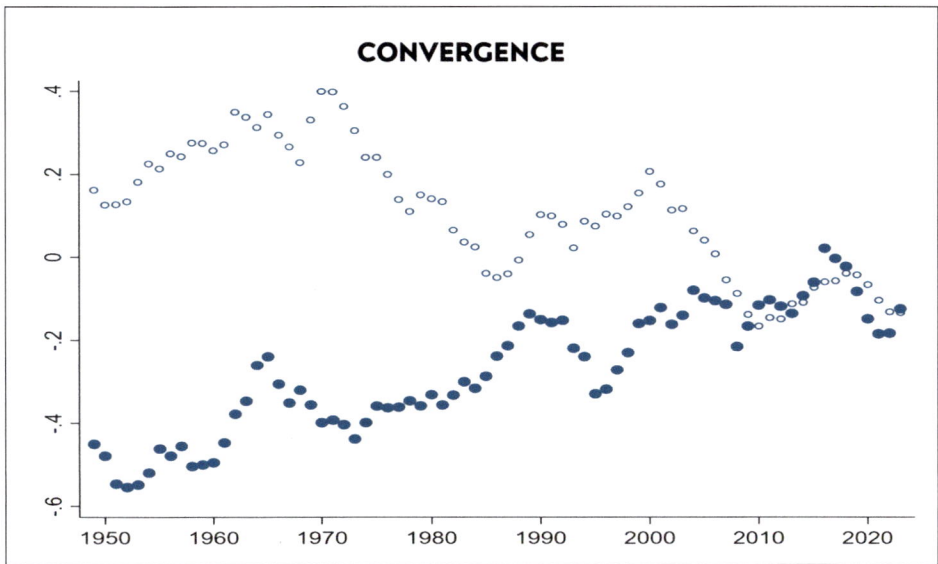

CONVERGENCE

Looking right around this period, where the trends shift, there is a regime change. A paper by Bob Ellickson and Bill Fischel looks at court fights about land use and zoning, where they talk about a kind of revolution and the restrictions that emerge over this time period. And the paper traces through how housing prices generate this trend change. What was going on in these two different periods in U.S. history postwar? What we are trying to do is relate this idea of directed migration—people moving to the richest parts of the country—to this idea of convergence. How could those two trends be related?

Think about a state with high wages and scarce labor. Then think about another state where wages are low. There are big returns for both high and low skilled workers if they move to the states with high wages and scarce labor. That migration should equilibrate levels. If you have one place with high skill levels, and one place where people have less education, and people can move around, you'll get convergence. If you have one pot of hot water, one pot of cold water, and people are free to move around, both pots converge towards each other. Directed migration could have been an important part of generating this convergence story. Then what happens when we stop building in the country's rich, productive areas? What happens when this regime of land use regulations starts restricting supply?

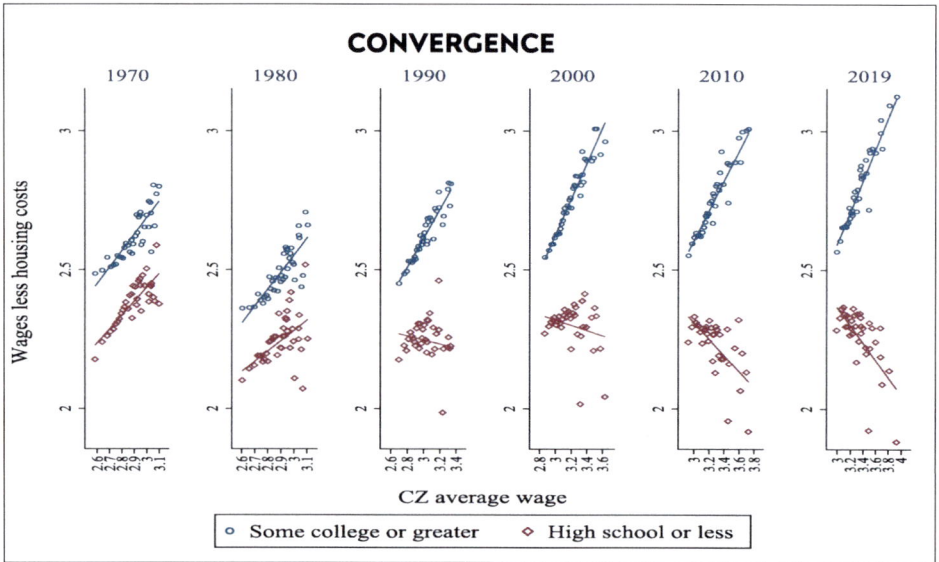

CONVERGENCE

1970 | 1980 | 1990 | 2000 | 2010 | 2019

Wages less housing costs (y-axis)

CZ average wage (x-axis)

○ Some college or greater ◇ High school or less

When building is restricted, housing prices start to become more important. That changes the return people receive from living in the country's richest regions. This chart shows commuting zones rather than states. Notice the average wages for those who went to college and those who did not in the 1970s. When you take the average wage and the commuting zone and you take the wage minus housing costs, both those who went to college and those who did not had higher wages after housing costs when they moved to richer areas.

If a bartender in Georgia is making \$9/hour he can move to San Francisco and significantly increase his income by making \$14/hour. As we stop building in the country's richest parts, however, the housing costs start to edge out the return for lower education workers. A bartender can make more in San Francisco versus Georgia, but not enough to pay the rent gap between those places.

By 2019, we still have average income across commuting zones: the richest commuting zones still offer higher wages after housing costs for college educated workers. But for non college educated workers, those returns are negative. It does not make sense to go from \$9/hour to \$14/hour by moving from Georgia to San Francisco because the rent increase mitigates the economic incentive. It turns out that even the wage gains for less skilled workers in these rich communities have decreased, never mind the housing costs.

What then is the problem with moving from a world where everyone—both high and low skilled workers—are moving to the richest parts of the country, to a world where moving only makes sense for high skilled workers? In our current world, it makes more sense for low skilled workers to move away from the richest areas. The result is what we see: there's huge disparity across U.S. states in all sorts of areas, not just productivity, but life expectancy, crime, obesity rates, and mobility. This is a serious challenge to dynamism.

PROGRESS
Figure 1. States Where Housing Supply Bills Passed in 2023, through June 30

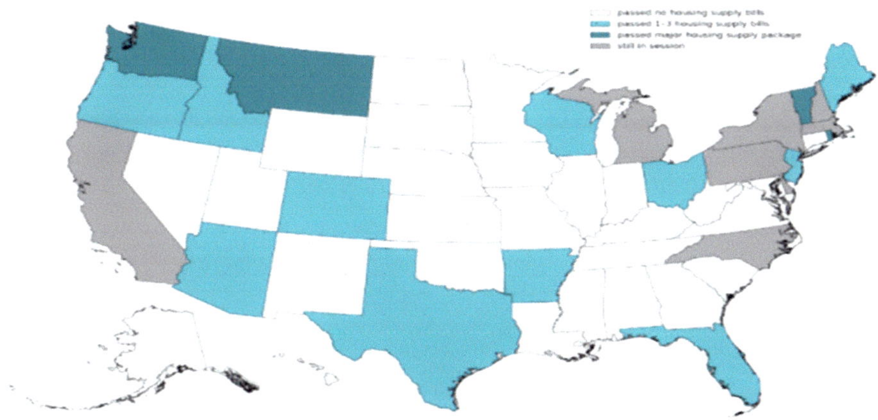

Source: Authors' tabulation and analysis. State boundary shapefile: IPUMS NHGIS, University of Minnesota, https://www.nhgis.org/

I have been talking a lot about this growing problem of restricting supply. The policy world has been increasingly recognizing this problem. Important reforms are starting to arise. Austin is a center point; there have been large reductions in parking requirements in Austin. Cities require builders to provide a certain number of parking spaces alongside every new project. The number in some places including Austin, Minneapolis, and Montana has decreased and required reduced lot sizes, but there is still much more to do.

I will now translate research into tools for use in policymaking. Here are examples of some of my projects where we work to make that happen.

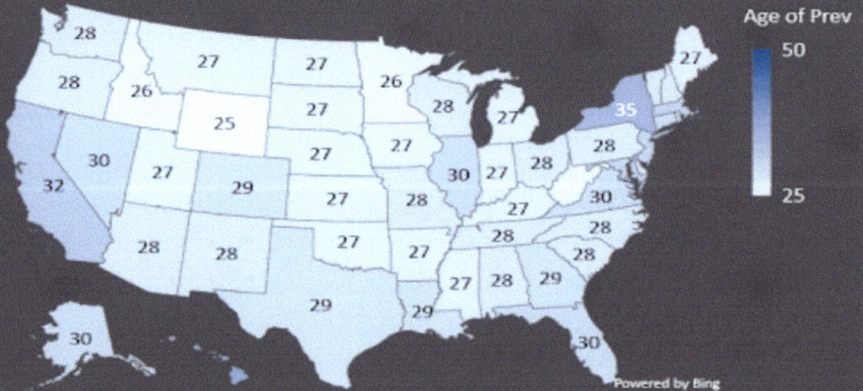

PROJECT 1: HOMEOWNERSHIP LADDER
1980

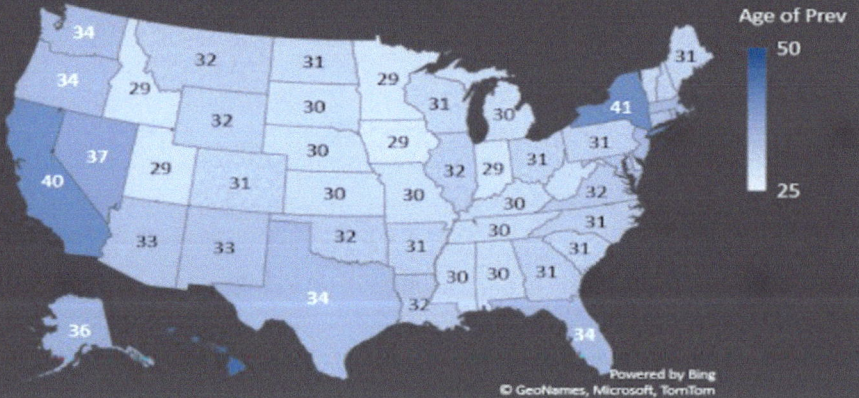

PROJECT 1: HOMEOWNERSHIP LADDER
2000

PROJECT 1: HOMEOWNERSHIP LADDER

2021

The first slide is the homeownership ladder, which looks at the age at which more than half of people own their homes. This is the age of prevalence. So around what age would you expect the median person to own their home? In 1980, at age 29, half of Texans owned their own home. By 2000, in Texas, that age is 34. By 2021, it's 37. And Texas is nowhere near the worst example. In California, the median age is 49 years old.

People recognize that this is happening. But is buying or not buying a home a policy issue? People are marrying later, they're staying the school longer, and having fewer children. Interest rates and financial considerations may plat a larger role in this major investment than we are considering. Should policymakers be worried about this? Is this entirely endogenous? How much are rising housing prices really causing this?

Economists measure the home ownership ladder as going from being a non owner to owning a home to owning a home free and clear. Not everyone follows the ladder, but it is the modal measurement. Instead of looking just at a home ownership ladder, we can think about an affordability ladder. Does one have the net worth to own a home? Do you have the net worth to own a home free and clear? Your personal decision to buy a home or not could depend on whether you decided to have kids and so forth but having the net worth to buy a home seems like an unambiguously good thing.

PROJECT 1: HOMEOWNERSHIP LADDER

Table 2: Alternative Affordability Scenarios and Their Impact on Homeownership Transitions

Scenario	Percent of the Decline in Ownership from 2000–2021 Potentially Avoided	Impact on Number of Californians Who Could Afford to Buy a Home
House Prices Rose Proportionately with Incomes	43%	637,378
House Prices Rose Proportionately with those in the Rest of the U.S.	48%	735,436
House Prices Rose Proportionately with Inflation	>100%	1,863,106

It is difficult to make causal statements about counterfactuals, such as how many more people would own a home if housing prices had played out differently, but the net worth calculator helps us bypass this problem. You can ask about somewhere like California, for example, where if housing prices had only risen proportionately with inflation, or proportionately with the rest of the United States, how much of the decline in home ownership affordability could we have avoided?

When thinking about whether a home is affordable, one must account for the traditional metric of cost burden. According to H.U.D., your cost burden is too high if you spend more than thirty percent of your income on housing. This is obviously imprecise. This assumption comes out of legislation, no economic arguments back it up, and it leads to crazy interpretations. An East Cleveland home is not unaffordable, merely because the people who live there spend more than thirty percent of their income on it. The recommendation ignores normal English by claiming that such properties are unaffordable and classifying them as cost burdens, even though they would classify Kim and Kanye's house as completely affordable because it costs far less than thirty percent of their income.

This problem arises because we are defining cost burden based on many different sorts of selection. It is true that the homes of people who buy in Beverly Hills might not be at a cost burden to them, but those buyers are heavily selected. People with normal incomes do not live there. We need a measure of affordability that undoes that selection. Selection has even another dimension: how large is the house your money gets you? It may be true that in San Francisco's Mission District, you can buy a studio for around $600,000. With that somewhat low average sale price, however, you get an unreasonably small property. How can we account for this selection?

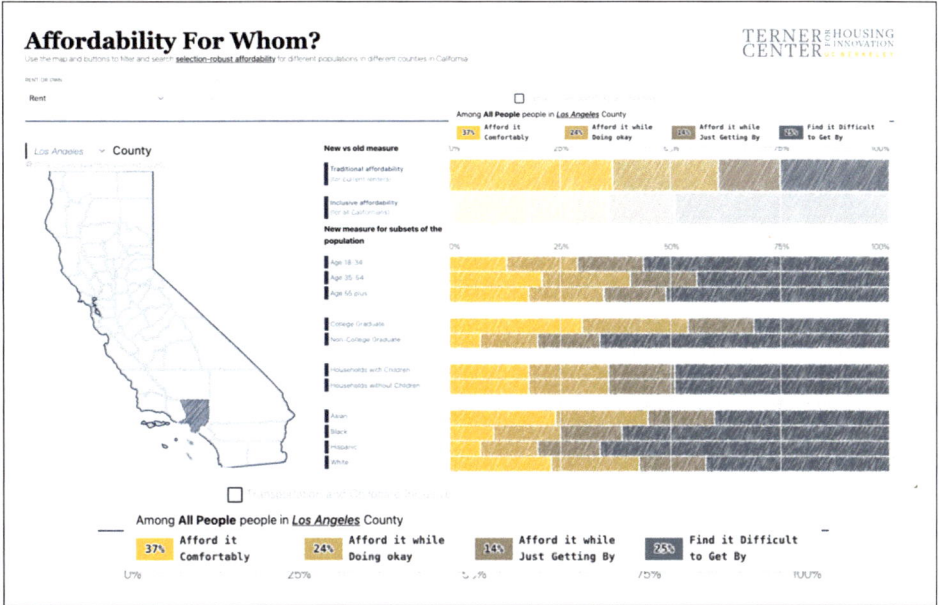

Another one of my projects with the Terner Center Project in California is building a tool for a selection-robust version of affordability. You can select Los Angeles County, for example. What percent of all Californians, or all Californians 18-34, or all college graduates could afford to rent in L.A.?

How do we produce these numbers? First, take a target population. Based on family size you can calculate the size of the home they would need to buy, the prices in the target location, and then project wages based on wage premium in the target location. And then you can produce measures of affordability not just for people who currently live in Beverly Hills where it may look affordable because of the people who live there but based on counterfactual populations. You can calculate how affordable Beverly Hills is, not just for Kim and Kanye, but for everyone—all Californians or all Americans or all college graduates. When you're thinking about finding measures of affordability, building tools like this can be helpful for policymakers, as opposed to trying to use conventional, somewhat misleading tools.

The last project I want to talk to you about is how we can take academic work on regulations and create concrete tie-ins to development. Sometimes researchers invent measures of regulation, like land use cases, that are not helpful. Measuring regulation in this way means nothing to a developer who thinks in terms of floor area ratio, parking requirements, setbacks, maximum height, etc. Academic researchers often take regressions of individual rules and look at statistical relationships between them. That is not always helpful because there are many kinds of complicated interactions between them. Increasing a building's maximum height requirement without changing the floor to area ratio means that the original change will have no effect. Or changing the floor area ratio but make the change in a location where there is little demand

PROJECT 3: DEVELOPMENT DASHBOARD

Land Use Cases Per Million People

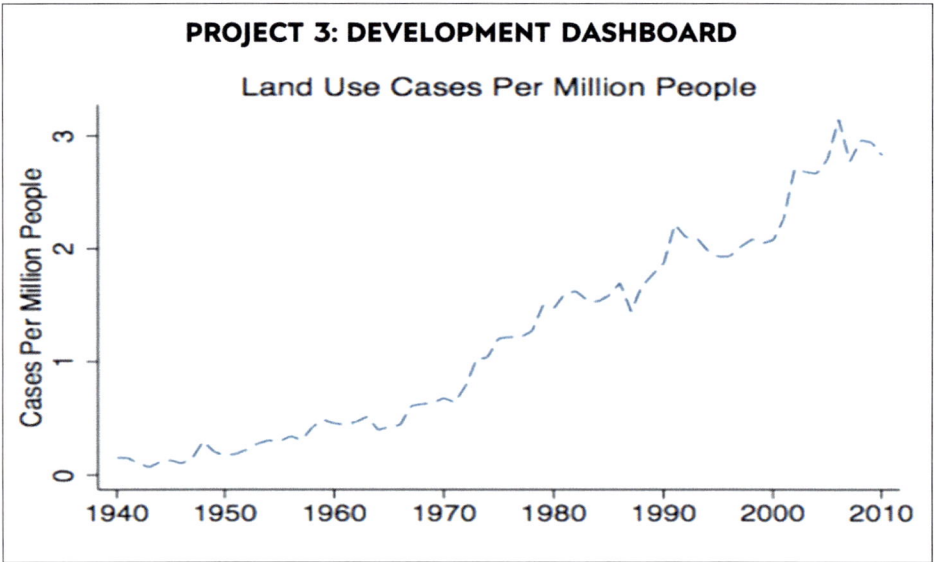

could also have no effect.

The relationship between all these different rules is nonlinear and interdependent. The results of changing them piecemeal are situations where you change one regulation and expect everything to improve, but it turns out it was the other regulation that was binding. This happened in Minneapolis. What can you do with this? Developers are putting these regulations into a pro-forma profitability analysis. When developers are trying to decide whether to build, they map out how much rent to expect, what development costs will be, how much time it will take to get permits, how many parking spaces they will have to provide, maximum height requirements, where curb cut-outs will be, etc. I have been working with the Terner Center to take a parcel-by-parcel, pro-forma profitability analysis based on factors like how many parking spaces per unit a new development will need or how long it will take to get a permit.

PROJECT 3: DEVELOPMENT DASHBOARD

For each parcel in San Francisco or in Los Angeles, for example, you can figure out whether it will be profitable to build or redevelop one unit, two units, three units, or four units, and what is legal to build based on the restrictions. The tool calculates a probability that developers will decide to build in that area. You can make this calculation historically. You can choose a parcel in 2010, for example, and see whether this kind of profitability analysis forecasts over the last ten years. It does. It's not surprising, because people like to make profits.

What can you do with this data? Well, now you can analyze changing regulations, not in some broad statistical average—reducing the number of parking spaces, for example, in some unhelpful average where sometimes it matters and sometimes it does not—but at a personal-by-personal level and work through all these different interactions.

This is the sort of information that could positively affect policy. In California, cities must submit housing elements that are supposed to meet their regional housing need requirements. This opened a certain number of plots for development. But not every plot has the same likelihood to open for development. You could imagine framing legislation in terms of expected number of new units.

When you think about a cost burden and affordability, you think about area median income. You think about standards for median income or low income in Santa Clara County, where median income is $181,000. That means you can be a family of four making well over $100,000 and be in the low-income bracket. That is not wrong if you are taking a cost burden approach, but we might want to think about having these other dimensions of definitions.

This kind of work can affect policy and researchers are doing interesting and important work that could feed into this. There is a large project in the works to try to use A.I. or machine learning—text parsing—to look through zoning codes to develop broader datasets than those we've been able to get just with survey data. One of the projects I am working on currently looks at these widely used economic impact models which are based on input-output frameworks, trying to project effects. It is very theory oriented as opposed to based on data.

There is a lot that we can do in that area. The reason I spent a good part of my time talking about this is I think this can be the kind of information that can nicely bridge academia and policy. There is a movement that is interested in working on this problem. Going from a purely academic paper to a clickable tool that that you could use to forecast development or measure affordability is the kind of project where you can really get value outside of traditional academic department work.

Acknowledgements

I would like to thank our six contributors for the time they gave to preparing for and participating in the first Austin Symposium on dynamism. The quality of their work and their intellectual leadership in their respective fields is inimitable.

I would like to thank Lillian Mills, dean of the McCombs School of Business at the University of Texas at Austin, for co-hosting the symposium, and Tom Wiseman, the chair of the economics department, for co-hosting the symposium luncheon featuring Edmund Phelps.

Civitas Institute events coordinator, Melissa Pardue, ensured the symposium met the highest standards, and chief of staff, Sydney Leary, kept all the moving parts of the symposium and follow-up publication on track and on time. Civitas public affairs director, Bo Herlin, has overseen the publication of this volume, senior project manager, Allison Smythe, has managed the design, and editor, Lindsay Eberhardt, smoothed and clarified the presentations into the current chapters. Ethan Webman produced both the symposium video and the promotional video shorts.

~ Ryan Streeter